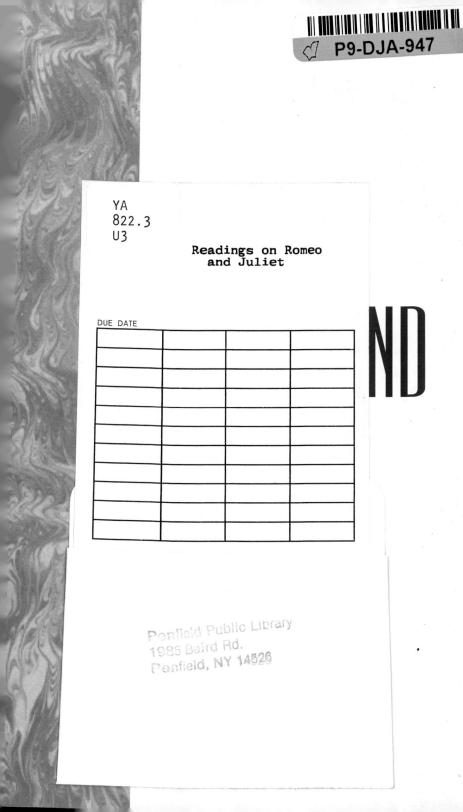

Readings on Romeo
and Juliet

ND

Other titles in the Greenhaven Press Literary Companion Series:

American Authors

Maya Angelou
Stephen Crane
Emily Dickinson
William Faulkner
F. Scott Fitzgerald
Nathaniel Hawthorne
Ernest Hemingway
Herman Melville
Arthur Miller
Eugene O'Neill
Edgar Allan Poe
John Steinbeck
Mark Twain

British Authors

Jane Austen
Joseph Conrad
Charles Dickens

World Authors

Fyodor Dostoyevsky
Homer
Sophocles

American Literature

The Great Gatsby
Of Mice and Men
The Scarlet Letter

British Literature

Animal Farm
The Canterbury Tales
Lord of the Flies
Shakespeare: The Comedies
Shakespeare: The Sonnets
Shakespeare: The Tragedies
A Tale of Two Cities

World Literature

Diary of a Young Girl

THE GREENHAVEN PRESS
Literary Companion
TO BRITISH LITERATURE

READINGS ON

ROMEO AND JULIET

David Bender, *Publisher*
Bruno Leone, *Executive Editor*
Brenda Stalcup, *Managing Editor*
Bonnie Szumski, *Series Editor*
Don Nardo, *Book Editor*

Greenhaven Press, San Diego, CA

Library of Congress Cataloging-in-Publication Data

Readings on Romeo and Juliet / Don Nardo, book editor.
        p.   cm. — (The Greenhaven Press literary
    companion to British literature)
    Includes bibliographical references and index.
    ISBN 1-56510-647-4 (lib. bdg. : alk. paper). —
ISBN 1-56510-646-6 (pbk.)
    1. Shakespeare, William, 1564–1616. Romeo and
Juliet. 2. Tragedy. I. Nardo, Don, 1947–   . II. Series.
PR2831.R43   1998
822.3'3—dc21   97-10491
                                                        CIP

Cover photo: Archive Photos

Copyright ©1998 by Greenhaven Press, Inc.
PO Box 289009
San Diego, CA 92198-9009
Printed in the U.S.A.

ROMEO: *For my mind misgives*

Some consequence, yet hanging in the stars,

Shall bitterly begin his fearful date

With this night's revels and expire the term

Of a despised life, closed in my breast,

By some vile forfeit of untimely death.

But He that hath the steerage of my course

Direct my sail!

—— *Shakespeare,* **Romeo and Juliet**

CONTENTS

Chapter 1: The Plot, Structure, and Characters of *Romeo and Juliet*

Discounting this argument, another critic here suggests that the tragic events of the play are character driven, particularly by those characters who act too quickly without weighing the potential negative consequences of their deeds.

Chapter 2: Themes and Ideas Developed in *Romeo and Juliet*

also have acted the role of Juliet's intended husband, Paris. This practice of character "doubling," common in Elizabethan theater, demanded that writers and directors work out elaborate staging schemes to allow enough time for one man playing multiple parts to change costumes.

FOREWORD

"'Tis the good reader that
makes the good book."

Ralph Waldo Emerson

The story's bare facts are simple: The captain, an old and scarred seafarer, walks with a peg leg made of whale ivory. He relentlessly drives his crew to hunt the world's oceans for the great white whale that crippled him. After a long search, the ship encounters the whale and a fierce battle ensues. Finally the captain drives his harpoon into the whale, but the harpoon line catches the captain about the neck and drags him to his death.

A simple story, a straightforward plot—yet, since the 1851 publication of Herman Melville's *Moby-Dick*, readers and critics have found many meanings in the struggle between Captain Ahab and the whale. To some, the novel is a cautionary tale that depicts how Ahab's obsession with revenge leads to his insanity and death. Others believe that the whale represents the unknowable secrets of the universe and that Ahab is a tragic hero who dares to challenge fate by attempting to discover this knowledge. Perhaps Melville intended Ahab as a criticism of Americans' tendency to become involved in well-intentioned but irrational causes. Or did Melville model Ahab after himself, letting his fictional character express his anger at what he perceived as a cruel and distant god?

Although literary critics disagree over the meaning of *Moby-Dick*, readers do not need to choose one particular interpretation in order to gain an understanding of Melville's novel. Instead, by examining various analyses, they can gain numerous insights into the issues that lie under the surface of the basic plot. Studying the writings of literary critics can also aid readers in making their own assessments of *Moby-Dick* and other literary works and in developing analytical thinking skills.

The Greenhaven Literary Companion Series was created with these goals in mind. Designed for young adults, this unique anthology series provides an engaging and comprehensive introduction to literary analysis and criticism. The essays included in the Literary Companion Series are chosen for their accessibility to a young adult audience and are expertly edited in consideration of both the reading and comprehension levels of this audience. In addition, each essay is introduced by a concise summation that presents the contributing writer's main themes and insights. Every anthology in the Literary Companion Series contains a varied selection of critical essays that cover a wide time span and express diverse views. Wherever possible, primary sources are represented through excerpts from authors' notebooks, letters, and journals and through contemporary criticism.

Each title in the Literary Companion Series pays careful consideration to the historical context of the particular author or literary work. In-depth biographies and detailed chronologies reveal important aspects of authors' lives and emphasize the historical events and social milieu that influenced their writings. To facilitate further research, every anthology includes primary and secondary source bibliographies of articles and/or books selected for their suitability for young adults. These engaging features make the Greenhaven Literary Companion series ideal for introducing students to literary analysis in the classroom or as a library resource for young adults researching the world's great authors and literature.

Exceptional in its focus on young adults, the Greenhaven Literary Companion Series strives to present literary criticism in a compelling and accessible format. Every title in the series is intended to spark readers' interest in leading American and world authors, to help them broaden their understanding of literature, and to encourage them to formulate their own analyses of the literary works that they read. It is the editors' hope that young adult readers will find these anthologies to be true companions in their study of literature.

INTRODUCTION

William Shakespeare's *Romeo and Juliet* is among the most widely recognizable and most often read and studied Western literary classics. A major reason for the play's continuing appeal is that its characters explore and express a wide range of human emotions and experiences, especially those that deal with young love. And nearly everyone who has read or watched the play—people of diverse backgrounds, cultures, and generations—has recognized and empathized with the feelings of the young lovers. As scholar John Erskine points out, Romeo and Juliet, as Shakespeare drew them, "illustrate a universal experience in a manner which, with all differences of time and language, is still universally understood. . . . To understand *Romeo and Juliet* is the common gift of lovers."

At the same time, in a profound sense Shakespeare's tale of "star-crossed" lovers has, at least in the Western world, helped to define the very meaning of romantic love. "The force of an overwhelming love that purifies and matures the protagonists [main characters]," maintain respected Shakespearean scholars Louis Wright and Virginia LaMar,

> is the dominant theme of *Romeo and Juliet*, and for more than three and a half centuries sentiments in this play have exerted a romantic influence upon countless readers. The probability is that it has subtly affected the attitude of the English-speaking peoples toward love. . . . Generations of young people have felt a deep emotional response to the play. It has been a part of nearly every literate person's emotional experience. At some point in his youth, nearly every man has idealized a Juliet no whit less glorious than the heroine of the play. Doubtless every girl has also seen herself as the object of such transcendent affection as Romeo's.

Indeed, the far-reaching cultural appeal and influence of literature's most famous lovers has always extended beyond the limits of classrooms and academic circles. *Romeo and Juliet* has been translated into nearly every known language, memorized, recited, quoted, and read for both pleasure and inspiration. And of course, fulfilling its author's original, primary intention, it has been performed countless times on the stage by some of the world's greatest actors and actresses. In addition, the play has seen new theatrical and dramatic life in numerous film versions (the latest released in 1996), as well as in fresh and bold modern reinterpretations, such as the Broadway musical *West Side Story*, in which the Shakespearean lovers are transformed into Tony and Maria, aligned with rival street gangs in twentieth-century New York City. Thus, Romeo and Juliet and their "story of woe" remain, and in all likelihood will always remain, popular icons symbolizing some of the deepest and strongest of human emotions.

The essays selected for the Greenhaven Literary Companion to Shakespeare's *Romeo and Juliet* provide teachers and students with a wide range of information and opinion about the play and its author's style, themes, and outlook on the human condition. All of the authors of the essays are or were (until their deaths) noted English-language experts, professors at leading colleges and universities, and/or scholars specializing in Shakespearean studies. Among this companion volume's several special features: Each of the essays explains or discusses in detail a specific, narrowly focused topic; the introduction to each essay previews the main points; and inserts interspersed within the essays exemplify ideas expressed by the authors, offer supplementary information, and/or add authenticity and color. Inserts are drawn from *Romeo and Juliet* or other plays by Shakespeare, from critical commentary about these works, and from other scholarly sources.

Above all, this companion book is designed to enhance the reader's understanding and enjoyment of the first of Shakespeare's great, timeless tragedies, a work that showed that even as a young man he possessed profound insights into the human condition. As the late and highly respected theatrical producer and Shakespearean authority Harley Granville-Barker put it in a 1934 essay about Shakespeare's dramatic art:

> With *Romeo and Juliet*, we find Shakespeare definitely set towards his end—which is, indeed, the end of all drama—the projection of character in action. And his advance will be to an ever deeper, richer, subtler conception and expression of character; finally also, to reflection in a man's expressions of himself of the world in which he spiritually dwells.

Biography: Romeo, Juliet, and the Man Who Made Them Immortal

It was the evening of October 17, 1935, at London's prestigious New Theater, where hundreds of expectant playgoers had gathered to witness the opening night of a new production of *Romeo and Juliet*. The curtain went up on a set representing a street in Verona, Italy, where the play's action takes place, and the spectators watched quietly as the actors playing Sampson and Gregory, servants of the house of Capulet, entered and conversed. A string of familiar events followed: the entrance of some servants from the rival house of Montague, their street brawl with the Capulet men, its escalation as others from the houses, including the lords themselves, joined the fray, and finally the intervention of Verona's prince, who lectured them about disturbing the peace. Through all of this, the audience sat quietly and patiently.

Then came the first entrance of one of the play's principals—Romeo—and at the mere sight of him a wave of sighs, gasps, and murmurs suddenly rippled through the audience. Witnesses would later write that the actor "came on looking every inch an Italian Renaissance prince . . . his gestures restless with the impetuosity of hot-headed youth," giving a vivid impression "of confused, impulsive, romantic adolescence, with much romantic subtlety of detail"; that he somehow seemed to have "the warm sun of Italy in his face and veins"; and that when he spoke he "caressed certain phrases" like "no other player in remembrance." As the performance continued, the young man continued to captivate the spectators. His reading of the line, "My mind misgives some consequence, yet hanging in the stars," which foreshadows the tragedy to come, was especially poignant; and his approach to the famous balcony scene moved one person to remark, "He stands against the balcony with such an extraordinary pose that [feelings of] animal magnetism and vitality and passion come right over."

The young actor playing Romeo that night was Laurence Olivier, whom critics and fellow actors would later acclaim as the greatest actor of the twentieth century. His presence in the cast, as well as that of the great English actor John Gielgud, who played Romeo's friend Mercutio, helped to propel the production through 186 performances, the longest single run of the play on record since its premiere over three centuries before.

Yet in spite of the brilliance of its lead players and its long and memorable run, the New Theater production of *Romeo and Juliet* was not the only highly acclaimed version of modern times, nor the most famous and popular. In addition to literally thousands of professional and amateur stage productions, four major films of the play have been released (in 1936, 1954, 1968, and 1996). The work's widespread popularity and appeal can be attributed to its long-standing reputation as one of the greatest love stories of all time, with title characters who are among the most recognizable romantic figures in world literature. Indeed, had the play been the sole work of its author, William Shakespeare, his place in the pantheon of Western literary greats would have been assured.

Of course, *Romeo and Juliet* was *not* the only play Shakespeare wrote, nor the best (most critics rank *King Lear, Hamlet,* and a few others higher), which makes his contribution to literature, theater, and culture in general that much more remarkable. "Shakespeare's works," writes Harvard University's noted Shakespearean authority Harry Levin,

> have ... been accorded a place in our culture above and beyond their topmost place in our literature. They have been virtually canonized as humanistic scriptures, the tested residue of pragmatic [practical] wisdom, a general collection of quotable texts and usable examples. Reprinted, reedited, commented upon, and translated into most languages, they have preempted more space on the library shelves than the books of—or about—any other author. Meanwhile, they have become a staple of the school and college curricula, as well as the happiest of hunting grounds for scholars and critics.

Shortly after Shakespeare's death, his contemporary, the renowned English poet and dramatist Ben Jonson, summed it up in a single phrase: "He was not of an age, but for all time!"

A UNIQUE TIME AND PLACE TO BE BORN

Jonson spoke of Shakespeare the writer, a poet for all ages. But what of Shakespeare the man in his own age? It is a common misconception that his life is largely mysterious and undocumented; in fact, for a commoner of the Elizabethan period it is unusually *well* documented. The evidence consists of more than a hundred official documents, including entries about him and his relatives in parish registers and town archives, legal records involving property transfers, and business letters to or about him; as well as more than fifty allusions to him and his works in the published writings of his contemporaries. These sources do not tell us much about Shakespeare's personality, likes and dislikes, and personal beliefs. Yet they provide enough information to piece together a concise outline of the important events of his life.

Shakespeare was born in Stratford, now called Stratford-on-Avon, a village in Warwickshire in central England, in 1564. The exact day is somewhat uncertain but tradition accepts it as April 23. If this dating is indeed correct, it is an unusual coincidence, for April 23 is celebrated in England as St. George's Day, in honor of the country's patron saint, and is also the documented month and day of Shakespeare's death fifty-two years later.

It seems fortunate for both Shakespeare and later generations that his birth and upbringing took place in England in the last decades of the sixteenth century. This particularly unique and crucial time and place supported one of the richest, most dynamic, and most opportune cultural and professional settings for aspiring poets and dramatists in all of Western history. Columbia University scholar Leonard Jenkins comments:

> Such famous writers as Francis Bacon, Christopher Marlowe, Ben Jonson, and John Donne were all born within a dozen years of Shakespeare's birth, and were publishing during his lifetime. The drama was just being recognized as a legitimate art form, and the first public theater [in England] was erected when Shakespeare was twelve. [Raphael] Holinshed's *Chronicles of England, Scotland, and Ireland,* the source for many of Shakespeare's plots, was published only shortly after that. During Shakespeare's lifetime many events of historical importance occurred. France gave sanction to Protestantism; England made peace with Spain; the colony of Jamestown in Virginia was formed; Puritanism, with its moralistic disap-

proval of the theater, grew in strength; and the King James Bible appeared.... [Amid all of this] the growingly recognized art of the theater provided fertile ground for the efforts and innovations of a young playwright, and the dramatic art was taken up by many and developed at an explosive rate.

YOUTH AND EDUCATION

That Shakespeare would become an important contributor to and shaper of this new and growing theater world was not at all apparent at first. At the time of his birth his father, John Shakespeare, was a glover and perhaps also a wool and leather dealer in Stratford, which was far away from bustling, cosmopolitan London, where most actors, writers, and other artists congregated and worked. The elder Shakespeare also held various local community positions, among them ale taster, town councilman, town treasurer, and eventually bailiff, or mayor. John and his wife, Mary Arden, were married shortly before the accession of Elizabeth I to the English throne in 1558; and they subsequently produced eight children, of whom William was the third child and eldest son.

Nothing is known about William Shakespeare's childhood, but it is fairly certain that between the ages of seven and sixteen he attended the town grammar school. There, students studied Latin grammar and literature, including the works of the Roman writers Terence, Cicero, Virgil, and Ovid, as well as works by later European authors such as the Dutch moralist Erasmus. In addition to these formal studies, Shakespeare must have done much reading on his own time in his teens and twenties. We know this because his works reveal a knowledge of—in addition to Latin, French, and several other languages—ancient history, particularly the *Parallel Lives* of the first-century A.D. Greek writer Plutarch; European history, as compiled by Holinshed and other English chroniclers; and European fiction, ranging from the Italian Boccaccio to the English Chaucer. Shakespeare also amassed a huge body of practical knowledge about life, including the ins and outs of the royal court, the trades, the army, the church, and the mannerisms and aspirations of people of all ages and walks of life. The eighteenth-century English novelist Henry Fielding described him as "learned in human nature"; therefore, Shakespeare was certainly a highly educated individual, even if most of what he knew was self-taught.

The first certainty about Shakespeare after his birth was his wedding, which his marriage license dates November 27, 1582. His bride, who was eight years his senior, was Anne Hathaway, the daughter of a farmer from the nearby village of Shottery. Local documents reveal a daughter, Susanna, christened May 26, 1583, and twins, Hamnet and Judith, christened February 26, 1585; other surviving records show that Hamnet died in 1596 at the age of eleven.

FORMATIVE YEARS IN THE THEATER

Why young Will Shakespeare chose the theater as a profession remains unknown. Traveling companies of actors came to Stratford occasionally, erected their makeshift wooden stages, and performed the most popular plays of the day. Stratford records indicate such visits from the theatrical troupes the Queen's Men and the Earl of Worcester's Men in 1568 and 1569, when Shakespeare was about five. Perhaps these and later stage shows he witnessed in Stratford intrigued him enough to send him to London to try his luck in the theater, an event that likely occurred in 1587, the year before the English defeated the Spanish Armada. Various undocumented stories have survived about the young man's first professional job, including one that maintains he tended horses outside a theater until offered the position of assistant prompter. "Another theory seems more likely," writes Shakespearean scholar François Laroque, namely that

> Shakespeare attached himself to a theatrical company—perhaps the Queen's Men, which happened to have lost one of its members in a brawl. The young Shakespeare could easily have stepped into his shoes, as experience was not required. Actors learned on the job.

Apparently Shakespeare learned more quickly than most. By 1593 he had written *Richard III, The Comedy of Errors,* and *Henry VI, Parts 1, 2,* and *3,* earning a solid reputation as a playwright and actor in the London theater scene. At first, he did not attach himself exclusively to any specific theatrical company, but worked on and off with several, including that of Richard Burbage, the finest and most acclaimed actor of the time. Burbage, four years younger than Shakespeare, became the playwright's close friend and colleague and eventually played the title roles in the original productions of some of his greatest plays, including *Hamlet, Richard III, King Lear,* and *Othello.* During these early years in London,

Shakespeare wrote two long poems, *Venus and Adonis* (1593) and *Lucrece* (1594), the only works he ever published himself. These works established him as a respectable literary figure; his plays, however, like those of other playwrights of the time, were viewed as popular but lowbrow entertainment rather than as legitimate literature.

An important turning point in Shakespeare's career was the formation in 1594 of the Lord Chamberlain's Men theatrical company, which performed at all the major theaters of the day, including the Theatre, the Swan, and the Curtain (the famous Globe had not yet been built). Shakespeare joined the group and stayed with it throughout his career. By 1603, renamed the King's Servants, the company was performing periodically at the royal court and Shakespeare was a shareholder in all company profits.

As a permanent member of the company, Shakespeare had the opportunity to work on a regular basis with the cream of English actors. In addition to the great Burbage, this elite included Henry Condell, John Heminge, William Sly, and Will Kempe. Kempe, one of the great comic players of the Elizabethan stage, specialized in broad, slapstick comedy and physical clowning. Evidence suggests that he played the role of Peter, the bumbling servant to the Nurse in *Romeo and Juliet*, and Dogberry, the constable in *Much Ado About Nothing*. Over the years Shakespeare wrote a number of comic roles especially for Kempe, among them Costard in *Love's Labour's Lost*, Launce in *The Two Gentlemen of Verona*, and Bottom in *A Midsummer Night's Dream*.

Indeed, from 1594 on Shakespeare devoted most of his time to writing plays, although he supposedly occasionally took small roles in productions of his and his colleagues' works (tradition has it that he played the Ghost in *Hamlet* and the old servant Adam in *As You Like It*). Between 1594 and 1601 his output was enormous and of astonishing variety and quality. A partial list includes the comedies *The Taming of the Shrew*, *The Two Gentlemen of Verona*, *The Merry Wives of Windsor*, and *Twelfth Night*; the histories *Richard II*, *Henry IV, Parts 1* and *2*, and *Henry V*; and the tragedies *Romeo and Juliet*, *Julius Caesar*, and *Hamlet*.

THE OPENING OF THE GLOBE

Incredibly, despite this relentless production of masterpieces, the playwright managed to find the time for journeys back and forth to rural Stratford and the family and community obligations centered there. In 1597 he became a local burgess, or council member, by buying New Place, the largest and finest home in the town (the property included two barns and two gardens); town records show that he later bought other property in the area, confirming that he had by then acquired more than what was considered a comfortable living at the time.

A significant portion of this large income must have come from Shakespeare's one-eighth share in the profits of the new and very successful Globe Theatre, which opened in 1598. He and his colleagues in the Lord Chamberlain's Men had found it difficult to renew their lease at the Theatre and had decided to build their own playhouse. In the short span of eight months they built the Globe on the south side of the Thames River and entered into a joint ownership deal with Sir Nicholas Brend, who owned the property; this marked the first known instance in theatrical history of actors' owning the theater in which they performed.

It was for this theater, which the best evidence suggests accommodated between two thousand and three thousand spectators, and the specific properties of its stage that Shakespeare tailored the plays he wrote in the years that followed. That stage, explains Levin,

> was basically a platform . . . [measuring] 27½ feet deep by 43 feet wide. . . . [It] was encircled on three sides by the standing spectators, or groundlings (who paid a penny for admittance), so that the production—if not quite in the round—employed what today we call arena staging. The surrounding amphitheater (apparently polygonal in the Globe) consisted of three stories, each with its gallery. . . . Admission to the galleries cost an additional penny and entitled the spectator to a seat. Just beyond [behind] the stage rose the tiring-house, containing—as the name (attiring house) implies—the actors' dressing rooms, and providing a conventionalized background which adapted itself to their histrionic requirements. Most of the acting had to take place downstage [toward the audience]; but upstage there was a curtained area which could be used for discoveries. . . . Behind its curtain, or arras, which was black for tragedy and parti-colored for comedy . . . would be discovered the body of the slain Polonius [in *Hamlet*] or the sleeping Falstaff [in *The Merry Wives of Windsor*], "snorting like a horse." In the back at a higher level, there was a specialized playing space indicated in the Shakespearean directions as "above" or "aloft.". . . There seem to have been practical upper windows, at one of which Juliet

first made her most celebrated appearance, in what later came to be known as the balcony scene. Somewhere beneath the windows, to the left and right of the mainstage, were the doors for major exits and entrances. Housed at the highest level were the musicians and the instruments for other sound effects that punctuated the dramatic rhythm. . . . The stage, which stood about five feet from the ground, could be entered from underneath by a trap or traps, whose most famous use was to serve for a grave for Ophelia [in *Hamlet*]. . . . Though the [theater's] large pit was open to the sky, most of the stage was covered by a projecting roof called the "shadow" or "heavens," whose underside was illuminated by signs of the zodiac. . . . Plays had to be performed in broad daylight, of course, between the hours of two and four or five in the afternoon. . . . Most of the attempted reconstructions err by making the Shakespearean playhouse look like a quaint little Tudor cottage, thatched and half-timbered. Actually . . . the Globe may have had arches, pilasters [pillars set into the walls], and other details of baroque architecture. When these were further embellished with bright hangings, costumed actors, and all the trappings of pageantry, the impression must have been spectacular.

Between 1600 and 1607, the Globe's open-air pit and arena stage were the scene of the premieres of most of what are now viewed as Shakespeare's greatest tragedies. These included *Hamlet, Othello, King Lear, Macbeth,* and *Antony and Cleopatra.*

SHAKESPEARE'S FINAL YEARS

The eight years that followed these monumental works were the playwright's last. Apparently now secure in his fame and fortune, he seems to have spent much of his time at New House in Stratford. There, according to various entries in local records and diaries, he became increasingly involved in community and family affairs. He still wrote plays, but no longer at the breakneck pace he had maintained in his youth. His last works included *Coriolanus, Pericles, The Winter's Tale, Henry VIII,* and *The Two Noble Kinsmen,* all first performed between 1608 and 1613. *Kinsmen* turned out to be his swan song. He must have become seriously ill in March 1616, for his will was executed on March 25; and he died nearly a month later on April 23. The bulk of his estate went to his wife, sister, and daughters Susanna and Judith, although he also left money to some of his theater colleagues, including Richard Burbage.

A few years after Shakespeare's death, a monument to

him, designed by Gerard Janssen, was erected in Stratford Church. A greater posthumous honor came in 1623 when two of his former theatrical partners, Henry Condell and John Heminge, published the so-called First Folio, a collection of the playwright's complete plays, under the title *Mr. William Shakespeare's Comedies, Histories, & Tragedies. Published According to the True Original Copies.* Exactly what these "copies" that served as the Folio's basis were is unclear; most scholars assume that they were various "quartos," early printed versions of the plays, which the actors often used as performance scripts. Whatever its sources, the First Folio was important because it included eighteen plays that had not already been printed in quarto form and that might otherwise have been lost to posterity. These included some of the playwright's greatest creations—*Julius Caesar, As You Like It, Macbeth, Antony and Cleopatra,* and *The Tempest.*

THE SOURCES FOR *ROMEO AND JULIET*

Romeo and Juliet was among those plays that appeared first in quarto versions and then in the First Folio. The version known as the First Quarto appeared in 1597; however, the play had by that time already been performed a number of times. The exact date Shakespeare wrote it is uncertain, but most scholars agree with an educated guess of about 1595. As a rule, he borrowed the bulk of the plots and many of the characters of his plays from existing sources, including ancient myths, historical accounts, popular stories, poems, novels, and so on; *Romeo and Juliet* is no exception.

The earliest known version of the story of young lovers from rival families meeting a tragic end was the ancient Greek myth of Pyramis and Thisbe (or Thisby). Determining to run away together, they plan a secret rendezvous; she arrives first, encounters a lion and runs away, dropping her cloak in the process; he arrives in time to see the lion mangling the cloak and, assuming she is dead, stabs himself; she returns later, finds his body and in despair uses the same knife on herself. Another important element of the familiar Romeo and Juliet story, namely that of a woman using a sleeping potion to avoid an unwanted marriage, first appeared in the novel *Ephesiaca* by the fourth-century A.D. Greek writer Xenophon of Ephesus.

In 1476 the Italian writer Masuccio of Salerno combined these ideas in a tale of star-crossed lovers published in his *Il*

Novellino. Scholar Joseph Kestner gives the following brief overview of this first Renaissance version of the story:

> Mariotto of Siena . . . [with] the aid of a Friar, secretly marries Gianozza. Having killed a man in a street fight, Mariotto is exiled to Alexandria [in Egypt]. As in *Romeo and Juliet*, the hero manages to have a final meeting with his wife before departing. Being forced into a marriage, Gianozza takes a sleeping potion concocted by the Friar. The Friar's message explaining the plot miscarries. Mariotto is arrested at the tomb and subsequently beheaded. His young widow enters a convent.

Masuccio's work was evidently a direct source for another Italian version, Luigi da Porto's *Istoria Novellamente*, written about 1530. Da Porto's story provided many now-familiar elements, including the setting of Verona in northern Italy, the names of the opposing families (Montecchi and Cappelletti), the balcony scene, the name of the male lover—Romeo—and his suicide by poison, and his sweetheart's suicide over his body.

Da Porto's work was very popular and widely imitated in the years that followed. Various versions included Italian Matteo Bandello's *Novelle* (1554), Frenchman Pierre Boaistuau's *Histoires Tragiques* (1559), and Englishman William Paynter's (or Painter's) *The Palace of Pleasure* (1567). Boaistuau's work was the direct source for English writer Arthur Brooke's 1562 poem *The Tragical History of Romeus and Juliet*, which was itself Shakespeare's immediate source for *Romeo and Juliet*.

Brooke's three-thousand-line poem has most of the plot elements and characters found in the play. But Shakespeare's changes, though seemingly slight, infuse the story with levels of irony, pathos, dramatic tension, and unbridled energy that propel it light-years beyond its predecessors and make it, hands down, the definitive version. For example, Shakespeare compresses events that take place over a span of nine months in Brooke's version into just a few days. In a single stroke this change makes the lovers' plight far more immediate, compelling, and suspenseful. Summing up Shakespeare's achievement in adapting the poem, scholar Frank Kermode, of University College in London, writes:

> To read Brooke with the play in mind is to be struck repeatedly by the easy skill with which Shakespeare has transformed the tale into a dramatic action, altering and compressing to make a sharp theatrical point, telescoping events, expanding such characters as the Nurse and Mercutio, cut-

ting material and inventing new episodes. The effect is not merely to make the story fit "the two hours' traffic of our stage"... but to display in it qualities of passion and intellectual subtlety hidden under the surface of other versions. There are echoes of word and image [from Brooke's version], and the run of the story is the same; Brooke must have his due. Yet the play, considered in relation to its source, is one of the dramatist's most brilliant transformations.

Thus, the greatness of Shakespeare's play lies not in its originality, but in its execution, which is unique. As his modern biographer Peter Quennell put it, "Shakespeare's tragedy is Shakespearean throughout; to any plumes he appropriated he gave a fresh and dazzling luster."

TEXTUAL PROBLEMS

Although we can trace the literary evolution of the story of the star-crossed lovers through the ages and marvel at the power and beauty of Shakespeare's version, it is now impossible to reconstruct the exact details of his original manuscript. In fact, none of his handwritten manuscripts have survived and post–First Folio editions of *Romeo and Juliet* have had to be pieced together from the early quartos. Because these came from different times and in some cases individual productions of the play, many words and speeches differ from one version to another. Scholars Louis Wright and Virginia LaMar, who edited the Folger Shakespeare Library's popular modern editions of Shakespeare's plays, here explain the problems they faced in preparing their text of *Romeo and Juliet:*

> The First Quarto version of 1597 is classified as a "Bad Quarto." That is, it seems to have been a pirated version, "reported" by one or more actors who remembered parts and reproduced the lines from memory as best as they could. Garbled and curtailed as some of the passages are, Quarto I has many readings that are better than those that appear in later texts.... This Quarto also contains a number of detailed stage directions not found in later editions.... The Second Quarto of 1599, "Newly corrected, augmented, and amended," is supposed to have been printed from a playhouse copy, and one would assume that it represents the authorized version insofar as there is one that had the sanction of Shakespeare's company.... A Third Quarto of 1609 was printed from the Second Quarto; the Folio version of 1623 and an undated Fourth Quarto follow the text of the Third Quarto. Yet all of these introduce some independent and occasionally improved readings. The best that a modern editor can do is to collate the ear-

lier versions and choose the readings that best represent the
meaning that was apparently intended. The analysis of the
text by the most skillful students of bibliographical science
cannot insure that a reading is Shakespeare's own or that it
does not represent some tinkering in the playhouse. No sanctity of Holy Writ attaches to Shakespeare's or to any other dramatic text in the Elizabethan period.

STRIKING IMAGES AND COLORFUL CHARACTERS

Nevertheless, while Wright, LaMar, and other scholars and
editors often quibble about details, all agree that the differences among the quartos are relatively slight when viewed
against the larger backdrop of the play as a whole. No one
disputes, for instance, that it is filled with striking imagery
and thematic development. The author's use of the image/
theme of light, for example, which appears in numerous
forms and various references throughout the play, is particularly noteworthy. In an early scene, torches and candle
clusters illuminate the Capulets' party, where the lovers first
meet; and after first catching sight of Juliet, Romeo exclaims, "O, she doth teach the torches to burn bright!" Later,
in the famous balcony scene, the lovers are bathed in bright
moonlight. When Romeo reveals himself to her, her first
shocked reaction is to compare his appearance to summer
lightning: "It is too rash, too unadvised, too sudden, too like
the lightning, which doth cease to be ere [before] one can
say 'It lightens.'" The lovers' meeting soon ends with the
dawn; and in their second balcony scene (act 3, scene 5),
dawn again draws them apart:

> ROMEO. Look, love, what envious streaks
> Do lace the severing clouds in yonder East—
> Night's candles are burnt out. . . .
> I must be gone and live, or stay and die.

> JULIET. Yond light is not daylight; I know it, I.
> It is some meteor that the sun exhaled
> To be to thee this night a torchbearer
> And light thee on thy way to Mantua. . . .
> [Suddenly acknowledging it is morning] It is, it is! . . .
> O, now be gone! More light and light it grows.

> ROMEO. More light and light—more dark and dark our woes!

These references to night giving way to dawn are among
several reminders in the play that life is inevitably punctuated and regulated by transformations from darkness to
light and back again, that people's lives are largely domi-

nated by larger forces they cannot hope to control. Reinforcing this theme of light versus darkness, the lovers' lives end, of course, in the dark recesses of a tomb, after which "the sun for sorrow will not show his face."

Indeed, one of the strongest thematic threads winding through the play is the influence of the stars and fate on humans, in this case particularly the lovers. In the Middle Ages and Renaissance, belief in astrology, holding that the stars and planets help direct people's lives, was widespread and strong. "Because it caused men to behave and react without knowing why," Leonard Jenkins explains, "this influence was regarded as a kind of fate." Parents who could afford it often called on astrologers to predict the temperaments and future fortunes, good or bad, of their newborn children. A common view was that fate and the stars had the power to override the deepest human emotions, as well as people's attempts to control their own lives. Thus, Romeo and Juliet are "star-crossed," their union fated, from their very births, to failure. References in the text to fortune, fate, and the stars abound, especially those of Romeo, who early on fears "some consequence, yet hanging in the stars," later recognizes that he is "fortune's foe," and later still, deciding to risk death to visit Juliet in the tomb, cries, "Then, I defy you, stars!"

Scholars also agree that *Romeo and Juliet* features colorful, unusually well defined characters who often display worldly or earthy qualities, insightful wit, and sensuous and bawdy humor. "Vivid poetry is wedded to brilliant characterization" in the play, state Wright and LaMar,

> and the action is rapid and tense. To give light and shade to the portrayal of the principal characters, Shakespeare includes minor figures whose words and actions supply contrast and color. Although he centers our interest upon the idealistic love of Romeo and Juliet, he provides contrasts in the characterizations of the ribald [vulgar] Mercutio, the materialistic ambitions of the matchmaking Capulets, and the Nurse's recollections of sensual pleasures. The comic parts are not overplayed and are just sufficient to give relief from tragic action that otherwise would keep the play at too high a tension.

A SMOOTH AND FLUID FLOW OF SCENES

In Shakespeare's own time, these qualities of imagery, theme, and characterization were considerably enhanced by the staging and presentation. For one thing, the Elizabethan stage, with its forward-thrusting arena platform, trapdoors, and multistoried, balconied galleries, was versatile and flexible, allowing the progression of scenes and scene changes to flow rapidly rearward and forward and up and down in an uninterrupted and fluid fashion. These scene transitions were accomplished without the aid of modern conventions such as lowering and raising a large curtain or dimming the lights (since the performances took place in midafternoon in an open-air playhouse and electric lights, of course, had not yet been invented).

Thus, for example, the sequence of four scenes that begins with act 3, scene 3 and ends with act 4, scene 1 might have progressed in the following way. Act 3, scene 3, in which Friar Laurence, Romeo, and the Nurse discuss the young man's impending banishment, takes place in the Friar's cell. A likely staging area for this enclosed space was the discovery area behind the small curtain at the rear of the stage. As Romeo bids the Friar farewell at the end of the scene, the curtain would close, just as Lord and Lady Capulet and young Paris enter the stage from one of the doors in the tiring house wall. The three would then play act 3, scene 4, a discussion about the match between Juliet and Paris, on one side of the stage. At the scene's conclusion, they would exit through the same door they entered from; simultaneously, Juliet and Romeo would appear on the balcony in the upper story of the tiring house, shifting the spectators' attention upwards for the start of act 3, scene 5. The audience was now supposed to imagine that this was the balcony outside of Juliet's bedroom overlooking the Capulets' orchard. Partway through the scene, the Nurse warns the lovers that Lady Capulet is about to enter. Romeo's only logical way out is through the orchard, so the actor probably climbed down a rope to the stage and slipped away, just as Juliet's mother appeared above on the balcony. After Lord Capulet makes his entrance and the heated discussion about the upcoming marriage ensues, the players would exit; and as they were doing so the discovery space curtain directly below them would open once again, revealing the Friar and Paris in the Friar's cell.

Complementing this quick and smooth flow of action, the physical properties of the stage and the accepted theatrical conventions of the day also allowed the playwright and actors to use powerful visual images to punctuate and reinforce imagery and thematic material hinted at in the lines.

Perhaps the most potent example in *Romeo and Juliet* was the overriding theme of love and death, of a potentially happy match marred by the hand of dark fate. Many scholars believe that on the Elizabethan stage this theme was hammered home by the powerful juxtaposition of the images of the marriage bed and the funeral bier. The interior of Juliet's bedroom would likely have been represented in the discovery space behind the curtain, clearly delineated by her bed. "In the final scene," Jenkins suggests,

> as Romeo breaks into the Capulet vault [tomb], the curtain [of the discovery space] would again be pulled back. There, on the inner stage, would lie Juliet in her coffin. If the coffin were placed where the bed had been, we would have a visual evocation [suggestion] of the imagery of love ending in a marriage of death. The Elizabethan stage was made for such effects.

TRIUMPH AND TRAGEDY

Beyond its plot, themes, imagery, colorful characters, and intriguing staging possibilities, *Romeo and Juliet* is, above all, a magnificent poetic expression. It is a play of deeply felt emotions—especially love and hate—which the characters readily translate into emphatic actions. Thus, the long-simmering feud between the Capulets and Montagues explodes into street brawling and leads eventually to the deaths of Mercutio and Tybalt; and Romeo and Juliet, smitten by a "prodigious birth of love," while fearful of their parents' intervention, rush headlong into a secret marriage that they do not realize is doomed from the outset. The emotions that drive these actions are universal and Shakespeare presents them in larger-than-life poetry that transcends time and place. This poetry lifts us, the audience, to a vantage from where we may view the pageant of the life, love, and death of the star-crossed lovers, of their triumph and tragedy, as it unfolds in its relentless way. And most importantly, through his verse Shakespeare shows us this tragedy in such a way that it does not drive us to despair and loss of all hope, but rather reassures us that true love, with the passionate and heroic feelings it inspires, is really possible after all. As scholar Northrop Frye puts it, "It takes the greatest rhetoric of the greatest poets to bring us a vision of the tragic heroic, and such rhetoric doesn't make us miserable but exhilarated, not crushed but enlarged in spirit."

CHAPTER 1

The Plot, Structure, and Characters of *Romeo and Juliet*

READINGS ON
ROMEO AND JULIET

The Story of the Star-Crossed Lovers

Charles and Mary Lamb

Charles Lamb was a renowned English poet, critic, and essayist who helped kindle an international nineteenth-century revival of interest in Elizabethan drama through his writings about Shakespeare and his contemporaries. In 1806 Charles and his sister, Mary, penned their now-famous *Tales from Shakespeare*, retellings of the stories of Shakespeare's most famous plays, their aim being to introduce these classics to English schoolchildren. The Lambs' beautifully rendered synopses soon became classics in their own right and have been frequently republished and widely read ever since. Following is a shortened version of their retelling of *Romeo and Juliet*, one of the saddest tales of tragic lovers in Western literature.

The two chief families in Verona were the rich Capulets and the Montagues. There had been an old quarrel between these families, which was grown to such a height, and so deadly was the enmity between them, that it extended to the remotest kindred, to the followers and retainers of both sides, insomuch that a servant of the house of Montague could not meet a servant of the house of Capulet, nor a Capulet encounter with a Montague by chance, but fierce words and sometimes bloodshed ensued. . . .

Old Lord Capulet made a great supper, to which many fair ladies and many noble guests were invited. All the admired beauties of Verona were present, and all comers were made welcome if they were not of the house of Montague. At this feast of Capulets, Rosaline, beloved of Romeo, son to the old Lord Montague, was present; and though it was dangerous for a Montague to be seen in this assembly, yet Benvo-

From "Romeo and Juliet," in *Tales from Shakespeare* by Charles and Mary Lamb (London, 1806).

lio, a friend of Romeo, persuaded the young lord to go to this assembly in the disguise of a mask, that he might see his Rosaline, and seeing her, compare her with some choice beauties of Verona.... To this feast of Capulets then young Romeo with Benvolio and their friend Mercutio went masked. Old Capulet bid them welcome, and ... they fell to dancing, and Romeo was suddenly struck with the exceeding beauty of a lady who danced there, who seemed to him to teach the torches to burn bright ... beauty too rich for use, too dear for earth! like a snowy dove trooping with crows (he said), so richly did her beauty and perfections shine above the ladies her companions. While he uttered these praises, he was overheard by Tybalt, a nephew of Lord Capulet, who knew him by his voice to be Romeo. And this Tybalt, being of a fiery and passionate temper, could not endure that a Montague should come under cover of a mask, to fleer [mock] and scorn (as he said) at their solemnities. And he stormed and raged exceedingly, and would have struck young Romeo dead. But his uncle, the old Lord Capulet, would not suffer him to do any injury at that time, both out of respect to his guests, and because Romeo had borne himself like a gentleman, and all tongues in Verona bragged of him to be a virtuous and well-governed youth. Tybalt, forced to be patient against his will, restrained himself, but swore that this vile Montague should at another time dearly pay for his intrusion.

The dancing being done, Romeo watched the place where the lady stood; and under favour of his masking habit ... he presumed in the gentlest manner to take her by the hand, calling it a shrine, which if he profaned by touching it, he was a blushing pilgrim, and would kiss it for atonement. "Good pilgrim," answered the lady, "your devotion shows by far too mannerly and too courtly: saints have hands, which pilgrims may touch, but kiss not."—"Have not saints lips, and pilgrims too?" said Romeo. "Ay," said the lady, "lips which they must use in prayer."—"O then, my dear saint," said Romeo, "hear my prayer, and grant it, lest I despair." In such like allusions and loving conceits they were engaged, when the lady was called away to her mother. And Romeo inquiring who her mother was, discovered that the lady whose peerless beauty he was so much struck with, was young Juliet, daughter and heir to the Lord Capulet, the great enemy of the Montagues; and that he had unknowingly engaged his heart to his foe. This troubled him, but it could not dissuade him from loving. As little rest had Juliet, when she found that the gentleman that she had been talking with was Romeo and a Montague, for she had been suddenly smit with the same hasty and inconsiderate passion for Romeo, which he had conceived for her; and a prodigious birth of love it seemed to her, that she must love her enemy, and that her affections should settle there, where family considerations should induce her chiefly to hate.

A VOICE IN THE GARDEN

It being midnight, Romeo with his companions departed; but they soon missed him, for, unable to stay away from the house where he had left his heart, he leaped the wall of an orchard which was at the back of Juliet's house. Here he had not been long, ruminating on his new love, when Juliet appeared above at a window.... And she, leaning her cheek upon her hand, he passionately wished himself a glove upon that hand, that he might touch her cheek.... She, unconscious of being overheard, and full of the new passion which that night's adventure had given birth to, called upon her lover by name (whom she supposed absent): "O Romeo, Romeo!" said she, "wherefore art thou Romeo? Deny thy father, and refuse thy name, for my sake; or if thou wilt not, be but my sworn love, and I no longer will be a Capulet." Romeo, having this encouragement, would fain have spoken, but he was desirous of hearing more; and the lady continued her passionate discourse with herself (as she thought), still chiding Romeo for being Romeo and a Montague, and wishing him some other name, or that he would put away that hated name, and for that name which was no part of himself, he should take all herself. At this loving word Romeo could no longer refrain, but taking up the dialogue as if her words had been addressed to him personally ... he bade her call him Love, or by whatever other name she pleased, for he was no longer Romeo, if that name was displeasing to her. Juliet, alarmed to hear a man's voice in the garden, did not at first know who it was ... but when he spoke again ... she immediately knew him to be young Romeo, and she expostulated with him on the danger to which he had exposed himself by climbing the orchard walls, for if any of her kinsmen should find him there, it would be death to him, being a Montague. "Alack," said Romeo, "there is more peril in your eye, than in twenty of their swords. . . . Better my life should be ended by their hate, than that hated life should be prolonged, to live without your love."—"How came you into this place," said Juliet, "and by whose direction?"—"Love directed me," answered Romeo. . . .

From this loving conference she was called away by her nurse, who slept with her, and thought it time for her to be in bed, for it was near to daybreak; but hastily returning, she said three or four words more to Romeo, the purport of which was, that if his love was indeed honourable, and his purpose marriage, she would send a messenger to him tomorrow, to appoint a time for their marriage, when she would lay all her fortunes at his feet, and follow him as her lord through the world. . . . At last they parted, wishing mutually sweet sleep and rest for that night.

HANDS JOINED IN MARRIAGE

The day was breaking when they parted, and Romeo, who was too full of thoughts of his mistress and that blessed meeting to allow him to sleep, instead of going home, bent his course to a monastery hard by, to find Friar Laurence. The good friar was already up at his devotions, but seeing young Romeo abroad so early, he conjectured rightly that he had not been abed that night, but that some distemper of youthful affection had kept him waking. . . . But when Romeo revealed his new passion for Juliet, and requested the assistance of the friar to marry them that day, the holy man lifted up his eyes and hands in a sort of wonder . . . thinking that a matrimonial alliance between young Juliet and Romeo might happily be the means of making up the long breach between the Capulets and the Montagues; which no one more lamented than this good friar, who was a friend to both the families. . . . The old man consented to join their hands in marriage.

Now was Romeo blessed indeed, and Juliet, who knew his intent from a messenger which she had despatched according to promise, did not fail to be early at the cell of Friar Laurence, where their hands were joined in holy marriage; the good friar praying the heavens to smile upon that act, and in the union of this young Montague and young Capulet to bury the old strife and long dissensions of their families.

The ceremony being over, Juliet hastened home, where she stayed impatient for the coming of night, at which time

Romeo promised to come and meet her in the orchard, where they had met the night before. . . .

DEATH AT NOONDAY

That same day, about noon, Romeo's friends, Benvolio and Mercutio, walking through the streets of Verona, were met by a party of the Capulets with the impetuous Tybalt at their head. This was the same angry Tybalt who would have fought with Romeo at old Lord Capulet's feast. He, seeing Mercutio, accused him bluntly of associating with Romeo, a Montague. Mercutio, who had as much fire and youthful blood in him as Tybalt, replied to this accusation with some sharpness; and in spite of all Benvolio could say to moderate their wrath, a quarrel was beginning, when Romeo himself passing that way, the fierce Tybalt turned from Mercutio to Romeo, and gave him the disgraceful appellation of villain. Romeo wished to avoid a quarrel with Tybalt above all men, because he was the kinsman of Juliet, and much beloved by her. . . and the name of a Capulet, which was his dear lady's name, was now rather a charm to allay resentment, than a watchword to excite fury. So he tried to reason with Tybalt . . . but Tybalt, who hated all Montagues as he hated hell, would hear no reason, but drew his weapon; and Mercutio, who knew not of Romeo's secret motive for desiring peace with Tybalt . . . with many disdainful words provoked Tybalt to the prosecution of his first quarrel with him; and Tybalt and Mercutio fought, till Mercutio fell, receiving his death's wound while Romeo and Benvolio were vainly endeavouring to part the combatants. Mercutio being dead, Romeo kept his temper no longer, but returned the scornful appellation of villain which Tybalt had given him; and they fought till Tybalt was slain by Romeo. This deadly broil falling out in the midst of Verona at noonday, the news of it quickly brought a crowd of citizens to the spot, and among them the old lords, Capulet and Montague, with their wives; and soon after arrived the prince himself, who being related to Mercutio, whom Tybalt had slain, and having had the peace of his government often disturbed by these brawls of Montagues and Capulets, came determined to put the law in strictest force against those who should be found to be offenders. Benvolio, who had been eyewitness to the fray, was commanded by the prince to relate the origin of it; which he did, keeping as near the truth as he could without injury to

Romeo, softening and excusing the part which his friends took in it. . . . The prince . . . on a careful examination of the facts, pronounced his sentence, and by that sentence Romeo was banished from Verona.

A Sentence More Terrible than Death

Heavy news to young Juliet, who had been but a few hours a bride, and now by this decree seemed everlastingly divorced! When the tidings reached her, she at first gave way to rage against Romeo, who had slain her dear cousin . . . but in the end love got the mastery, and the tears which she shed for grief that Romeo had slain her cousin, turned to drops of joy that her husband lived whom Tybalt would have slain. Then came fresh tears, and they were altogether of grief for Romeo's banishment. That word was more terrible to her than the death of many Tybalts.

Romeo, after the fray, had taken refuge in Friar Laurence's cell, where he was first made acquainted with the prince's sentence, which seemed to him far more terrible than death. To him it appeared there was no world out of Verona's walls, no living out of the sight of Juliet. . . . The friar bade him beware, for such as despaired (he said) died miserable. Then when Romeo was a little calmed, he counselled him that he should go that night and secretly take his leave of Juliet, and thence proceed straightways to Mantua, at which place he should sojourn, till the friar found fit occasion to publish his marriage, which might be a joyful means of reconciling their families; and then he did not doubt but the prince would be moved to pardon him, and he would return with twenty times more joy than he went forth with grief. Romeo was convinced by these wise counsels of the friar, and took his leave to go and seek his lady, proposing to stay with her that night, and by daybreak pursue his journey alone to Mantua; to which place the good friar promised to send him letters from time to time, acquainting him with the state of affairs at home.

That night Romeo passed with his dear wife, gaining secret admission to her chamber, from the orchard in which he had heard her confession of love the night before. . . . The unwelcome daybreak seemed to come too soon, and when Juliet heard the morning song of the lark, she would have persuaded herself that it was the nightingale, which sings by night: but it was too truly the lark which sang, and a discordant and unpleasing note it seemed to her; and the streaks of day in the east too certainly pointed out that it was time for these lovers to part. Romeo took his leave of his dear wife with a heavy heart, promising to write to her from Mantua every hour in the day. . . .

A DESPERATE REMEDY

This was but the beginning of the tragedy of this pair of star-crossed lovers. Romeo had not been gone many days, before the old Lord Capulet proposed a match for Juliet. The husband he had chosen for her, not dreaming that she was married already, was Count Paris, a gallant, young, and noble gentleman, no unworthy suitor to the young Juliet, if she had never seen Romeo.

The terrified Juliet was in a sad perplexity at her father's offer. She pleaded her youth unsuitable to marriage. . . . She pleaded every reason against the match, but the true one, namely, that she was married already. But Lord Capulet was deaf to all her excuses, and in a peremptory manner ordered her to get ready, for by the following Thursday she should be married to Paris. . . .

In this extremity Juliet applied to the friendly friar, always her counselor in distress, and he asking her if she had resolution to undertake a desperate remedy, and she answering that she would go into the grave alive rather than marry Paris, her own dear husband living; he directed her to go home, and appear merry, and give her consent to marry Paris, according to her father's desire, and on the next night, which was the night before the marriage, to drink off the contents of a phial which he then gave her, the effect of which would be that for two-and-forty hours after drinking it she should appear cold and lifeless; and when the bridegroom came to fetch her in the morning, he would find her to appearance dead; that then she would be borne, as the manner in that country was, uncovered on a bier, to be buried in the family vault; that if she could put off womanish fear, and consent to this terrible trial, in forty-two hours after swallowing the liquid (such was its certain operation) she would be sure to awake, as from a dream; and before she should awake, he would let her husband know their drift, and he should come in the night, and bear her thence to Mantua. Love, and the dread of marrying Paris, gave young Juliet strength to undertake this horrible adventure; and she took the phial of the friar, promising to observe his directions. . . .

On the Wednesday night Juliet drank off the potion. She had many misgivings. . . . But then her love for Romeo, and her aversion for Paris returned, and she desperately swallowed the draught, and became insensible.

DEATH BY POISON

When young Paris came early in the morning with music to awaken his bride, instead of a living Juliet, her chamber presented the dreary spectacle of a lifeless corse. What death to his hopes! What confusion then reigned through the whole house! Poor Paris lamenting his bride . . . but still more piteous it was to hear the mournings of the old Lord and Lady Capulet, who having but this one, one poor loving child to rejoice and solace in, cruel death had snatched her from their sight. . . . Now all things that were ordained for the festival were turned from their properties to do the office of a black funeral. . . . Now, instead of a priest to marry her, a priest was needed to bury her; and she was borne to church indeed, not to augment the cheerful hopes of the living, but to swell the dreary numbers of the dead.

Bad news, which always travels faster than good, now brought the dismal story of his Juliet's death to Romeo, at Mantua, before the messenger could arrive, who was sent from Friar Laurence to apprise him that these were mock funerals only. . . . Just before, Romeo had been unusually joyful and light-hearted. . . . And now that a messenger came from Verona, he thought surely it was to confirm some good news which his dreams had presaged. But when the contrary to this flattering vision appeared . . . he ordered horses to be got ready, for he determined that night to visit Verona, and to see his lady in her tomb. And as mischief is swift to enter into the thoughts of desperate men, he called to mind a poor apothecary, whose shop in Mantua he had lately passed. . . . He sought out the apothecary, who after some pretended scruples, Romeo offering him gold, which his poverty could not resist, sold him a poison, which, if he swallowed, he told him, if he had the strength of twenty men, would quickly despatch him.

With this poison he set out for Verona, to have a sight of his dear lady in her tomb, meaning, when he had satisfied his sight, to swallow the poison, and be buried by her side. He reached Verona at midnight, and found the churchyard, in the midst of which was situated the ancient tomb of the Capulets. He had provided a light, and a spade, and wrenching iron, and was proceeding to break open the monument, when he was interrupted by a voice, which by the name of *vile Montague,* bade him desist from his unlawful business. It was the young Count Paris, who had come to the tomb of Juliet at that unseasonable time of night, to strew flowers and to weep over the grave of her that should have been his bride. . . . Romeo urged Paris to leave him, and warned him by the fate of Tybalt, who lay buried there, not to provoke his anger, or draw down another sin upon his head, by forcing him to kill him. But the count in scorn refused his warning, and laid hands on him as a felon, which Romeo resisting, they fought, and Paris fell. When Romeo, by the help of a light, came to see who it was that he had slain, that it was Paris, who (he learned in his way from Mantua) should have married Juliet, he took the dead youth by the hand, as one whom misfortune had made a companion, and said that he would bury him in a triumphal grave, meaning in Juliet's grave, which he now opened: and there lay his lady . . . and near her lay Tybalt in his bloody shroud, whom Romeo seeing, begged pardon of his lifeless corpse, and for Juliet's sake called him *cousin,* and said that he was about to do him a favour by putting his enemy to death. Here Romeo took his last leave of his lady's lips, kissing them; and here he shook the burden of his crossed stars from his weary body, swallowing that poison which the apothecary had sold him. . . .

THE SCOURGE OF HEAVEN

For now the hour was arrived at which the friar had promised that she should awake; and he, having learned that his letters which he had sent to Mantua, by some unlucky detention of the messenger, had never reached Romeo, came himself, provided with a pickaxe and lantern, to deliver the lady from her confinement; but he was surprised to find a light already burning in the Capulet's monument, and to see swords and blood near it, and Romeo and Paris lying breathless by the monument.

Before he could entertain a conjecture, to imagine how these fatal accidents had fallen out, Juliet awoke out of her trance, and seeing the friar near her, she remembered the place where she was, and the occasion of her being there, and asked for Romeo, but the friar, hearing a noise, bade her come out of that place of death, and of unnatural sleep, for a greater power than they could contradict had thwarted their intents; and being frightened by the noise of people coming, he fled; but when Juliet saw the cup closed in her true love's hands, she guessed that poison had been the cause of his end, and she would have swallowed the dregs if any had been left, and she kissed his still warm lips to try if any poison yet did hang upon them; then hearing a nearer noise of people coming, she quickly unsheathed a dagger which she wore, and stabbing herself, died by her true Romeo's side.

The watch by this time had come up to the place. A page belonging to Count Paris, who had witnessed the fight between his master and Romeo, had given the alarm, which had spread among the citizens. . . . A great multitude being assembled at the Capulets' monument, the friar was demanded by the prince to deliver what he knew of these strange and disastrous accidents.

And there, in the presence of the old lords Montague and Capulet, he faithfully related the story of their children's fatal love, the part he took in promoting their marriage, in the hope in that union to end the long quarrels between their families: how Romeo, there dead, was husband to Juliet; and Juliet, there dead, was Romeo's faithful wife. . . .

And the prince, turning to these old lords, Montague and Capulet, rebuked them for their brutal and irrational enmities, and showed them what a scourge Heaven had laid upon such offences, that it had found means even through the love of their children to punish their unnatural hate. And these old rivals, no longer enemies, agreed to bury their long strife in their children's graves. . . . So did these poor old lords, when it was too late, strive to outdo each other in mutual courtesies; while so deadly had been their rage and enmity in past times, that nothing but the fearful overthrow of their children . . . could remove the rooted hates and jealousies of the noble families.

Shakespeare Simplified and Improved an Old Story

John Erskine

In this essay, former Columbia University English professor John Erskine identifies and discusses some of the changes that Shakespeare made in what was in his time already a common tale of tragic lovers. Periodically citing the immediate source, Arthur Brooke's poem *The Tragical History of Romeus and Juliet,* as well as other earlier stories of lovers, such as the Greek myths of Pyramis and Thisbe and of Hero and Leander, Erskine points out that Shakespeare's alterations were on the whole structurally quite simple; yet, taken together, these changes were so thematically and emotionally meaningful that they made his version of the story immortal. Indeed, Erskine contends, *Romeo and Juliet* is one of the prime examples of Shakespeare's profound ability to "set an old story right."

Even before Shakspere increased its beauty and widened its appeal, the tragedy of Romeo and Juliet was, if not a classic, at least a popular story. The cruder versions of it suggested some resemblance to the best ancient and medieval love-legends—for example, to the story of Hero and Leander, of Pyramus and Thisbe, of Tristram and Iseult [or Isolde], perhaps also of Troilus and Cressida; and in the continual re-handling of the theme by French and Italian paraphrasers and translators, these reminiscences of long remembered tales developed into unmistakable symptoms of immortality. Shakspere was dealing, therefore, with far richer material made ready to his hand when he meditated on Brooke's poem, or on other accounts of Romeo and Juliet, than when he studied Holinshed's record of Macbeth or Cinthio's dark

From "Romeo and Juliet" by John Erskine, in *Shakespearean Studies by Members of the Department of English and Comparative Literature in Columbia University,* Brander Matthews and Ashley H. Thorndike, eds. (New York: Columbia University Press, 1916).

tale of the Moor [Othello]. Yet in no other version than Shakspere's did this love-story enjoy a much larger audience, or
appeal to a much later time, than that which read it first.
Every known form of it, from Masuccio to Brooke, contained
some passing note, some temporary emphasis, which
clearly enough, as we can see now, narrowed and shortened
its fame.

If it is curious that a tale of such vitality should have
waited so long for an adequate rendering, it is still more extraordinary that in order to transfigure it into a world poem
Shakspere should have made so few and such simple
changes. In one sense, of course, his changes and additions
were large and momentous, for at a stroke he expressed ad-
equately for the race what it had long tried in vain to say.
But in another sense the changes were slight. In fact,
'Romeo and Juliet' illustrates better than some of his greater
dramas the essentially corrective quality in Shakspere's genius—the gift for setting an old story right, for adjusting it
to the criticism of facts, rather than for contriving novelties
and surprises. It might be argued that this play, though in
subject less complex and in many ways less profound, is a
happier instance than even 'Hamlet' of his genius for revis-
ing the labored inventions of other men into an obvious immortality; for Hamlet, even when clarified in Shakspere's
imagination, remains still a special case, arousing and baf-
fling our curiosity, whereas the two lovers, as he drew
them, illustrate a universal experience in a manner which,
with all differences of time and of language, is still universally understood. . . .

It is natural to ask by what changes, however slight, was
the story made to fit a universal experience. It is natural to
ask also whether something besides Shakspere's genius did
not contribute to the remarkable result. . . . As he tells the
story, it is far more simple than in the earlier versions; for
this difference his dramatic instinct may entirely account.
But the story is also far more innocent, and the characters
are more pure; and this difference makes of the play an essentially new drama, in spite of its far-descended plot, for
the innocence of the lovers appeals to certain emotions
which the Italian or French Romeo and Juliet could hardly
have aroused, and the appeal to these emotions has proved
as effective in Italy and France as in England and Germany.
To put the whole matter in a phrase, the story before Shak-

spere touched it was a tragedy which befell two young lovers; he made it the tragedy of young love.

LOVE'S FATAL BARRIERS

We may see more clearly the direction in which Shakspere simplified his plot if we first observe the contradiction which appears in all the great tragedies of love. Hero and heroine are doomed to love at the cost of whatever sacrifice, yet in circumstances which forbid their loving. Out of much experience of what is typical in passion, the race has chosen to remember chiefly that where the union of hearts seems most imperative, the barriers to it seem insurmountable.

If the form of this encounter between passion and its obstacles varies from story to story, we should expect as much, to parallel the changing definitions of love and of fate. . . . So in Romeo and Juliet the fated love meets the fatal barriers, though time has altered the terms of the paradox. Something more than youth and beauty or the fury of passion drew them to their doom. . . . They loved at first sight, as we say; and though the philosopher rightly reminds us now that in times when women were rarely seen and ordinarily not to be spoken to, people fell in love at first sight since they must fall in love somehow, yet the poet made something universal of that circumstance—with true lovers there seems to be no wooing, for they are mated ere they are born. The feud also, which was to defeat Romeo and Juliet with implacable hate, had been prepared for them before their birth. Their destiny was one passion, the obstacle to it was another.

This constant opposing of desire and disappointment in the great love-stories has inevitably suggested some relation between them, some migration of history or myth such as scholarship delights to trace. It is because of this conflict in all the stories that 'Romeo and Juliet' has been thought to show kinship with some of them—with the legend of Pyramus and Thisbe, for example, or of Hero and Leander, or of Tristram and Iseult. In all four instances, the lovers are separated; in each, the woman, finding the man dead or dying, kills herself. Yet the resemblances among the convincing tragedies of love probably spring from the disposition of love itself. It is not necessary to suppose that Shakspere studied these old tales, or even glanced hastily at them, as we have done, to recall the motions and attitudes of human passion; from experience and from observation he would know that to believe their passion authentic and obligatory is always the way of man and maid, whether they explain their persuasion of fate by the will of a goddess, or by the working of a magic draught [drink], or by a blessed recognition between affianced souls. That this world is not a hospitable place in which to realize the destinies of the heart, is naturally the second conviction of impatient love; the particular fate that speaks distinctly to lovers, society around them is always slow to hear. When the moral sense was crude, the high-handed suitor might well locate this social inhospitality in the protests of the lady's discarded husband, or in earlier and frankly buccaneering times he might assume an angry goddess, or several of them, to explain the husband's unreasonable sensitiveness. But ages nobler and more refined have discovered the world's unreadiness for love in the reluctance of unacquainted families to rush into each other's arms, even to the third and fourth cousin, with that abandon of enthusiasm which lovers think fitting. This coldness of the families Shakspere raised to the tragic menace of an ancient feud.

LOVE VERSUS HATE

An ancient hatred, a destined love—upon this irreconcilable conflict the poet focuses all the distracted interests of the story he inherited, and this concentration brings about his simplicity. To fill the tragedy with meaning for all young lovers, he had only to emphasize the estrangement of Romeo and Juliet from their environment; he therefore rearranged his material so as to bring out clearly three contrasts—the contrast of love with hate, of youth with age, of courtesy with vulgarity. The contrast with hate has often been analyzed, and it needs but a brief summary here. It shows itself in the old quarrel of the houses, so old that no one remembers how it began. The servants of the families fight in the streets till they become a public nuisance, yet the quarrel with them is mechanical. With Tybalt, however, it is quite conscious; the feud is stored up in him as pure venom, hate incarnate. As though to explain him, Shakspere makes the Capulets the quarrelsome family, whose hot temper and wilfulness center in this one unpleasant character. Juliet's sorrow for him is no deeper than kinship demands, and that her parents should think her to be grieving over his death is explicable only by their exaggerated clan loyalty. Yet though Shakspere clarifies the story by distinguishing between the temper of the families, he is too observing to set up an absolute or mechanical difference; he allows the Capulets, even Tybalt, a better self, a melting mood. To be sure, whether it is a servant or Tybalt himself, it is always a Capulet who begins the fight, whereas the Montagues, at least Romeo and Benvolio, are consistently for peace. Yet we too easily overlook the instances when the impulsive Capulets take a generous course. The one glimpse we have of the gentler Tybalt is, unfortunately for him, where few readers find it—in a silence. When he comes upon Romeo and challenges him to fight, angry because the Montague had dared to come uninvited to the Capulet banquet, the newly-married husband asks for his friendship instead of his hate, and Tybalt drops the quarrel. If Mercutio had not misunderstood Romeo's motive, and had not then provoked Tybalt on his own account, there might have been a chance of reconciliation. Tybalt's kindly moment, it should be noted, seems to be an invention of Shakspere's, one of his simple but important changes. In Brooke's poem Tybalt did not see Romeo at the banquet, and therefore had no cause to be angry with him, but challenged him merely for the sake of fighting, whereupon Romeo promptly slew him in self-defence. Shakspere specifies also that it was old Capulet who first confessed himself wrong and asked forgiveness at the grave of his child. Yet with all these shadings of character, the poet manages to concentrate every degree of malevolence in an almost visible cloud of death, which shadows the story from beginning to end, and which is felt quite naturally in the dark metaphors of the dialog. 'My only love sprung from my only hate,' says Juliet, when she learns who Romeo is. 'Where be these enemies?' asks the Prince ironically at the end of the play, when the two fathers look down at their dead children.

YOUTH VERSUS AGE

The estrangement of the children from their parents, which is suggested in the contrast between love and hate, is indicated sharply in the contrast between youth and age. The lovers are young, and in the story as Shakspere tells it only the young can sympathize with them. It is probably farfetched to think, with some readers, that the poet deliberately sounded the theme of youth in his metaphors, as he had sounded the theme of hate; it was probably in order to express Romeo's character rather than his own comment that he often gave the youthful lover a presentiment of evil, a sense of approaching death, which would seem but the humor of love melancholy did not the event give it tragic force. 'The game was ne'er so fair, and I am done,' he says, moping not for Juliet but for Rosaline. It is probably due to the exigencies of the plot rather than to any purpose of symbolism that the poet lays so many scenes at dawn or in the morning hours. We first hear of the sentimental Romeo as haunting the woods at dawn. It is in the morning that the first fight occurs. Romeo seeks Friar Laurence in his cell at dawn; at dawn he leaves Juliet, who is then told she must marry Paris; at dawn she is found apparently dead; at dawn she and Romeo and Paris are found in the tomb. Yet if these many sunrises are implicit in the story, it is otherwise clear that Shakspere knew the dramatic importance of the youth of the lovers. 'Wert thou as young as I,' says Romeo to Friar Laurence, 'then mightst thou speak.' Shakspere takes obvious pains to emphasize Juliet's youth by making her but fourteen years old, two years younger than she had been in earlier versions of the story; and he does more than name her years—he removes from her character every suggestion of experience with the world.

This morning-glamor in hero and heroine is set off by the age of their parents, age that has forgotten what love and youth are like. So violent has Shakspere made the contrast, that the tale seems to be of grandparents and grandchildren. 'Old Montague,' as Capulet calls him, cannot guess what ails Romeo, nor can Lady Montague, although the malady is too obvious to younger eyes for Benvolio not to hit it in his first question. . . . Shakspere makes Juliet's father so old that his best virtue is the patriarchal one of hospitality, and his wrath is petulant and senile. When he loses his temper, his wife reminds him none too politely that he had better call for a crutch than for a sword. . . .

As though to emphasize these master themes, these contrasts of love with hate, of youth with age, Shakspere announces them together in one consecutive passage, in the scene of Capulet's feast. It is always unsafe to ascribe to deliberate intention in Shakspere what may be only a coincidence, and it is not necessary to suppose that here the poet is conscious of all the irony in his lines; but those lines would hardly have been written had he not imagined the

story as in essence a conflict between love and its inhos-
pitable environment, between the immediateness of youth
and the forgetfulness of old age. Juliet's father, who represents Age, welcomes another Capulet to the feast, asks how
long it is since they two were 'in a mask,' and is astounded
to find it is thirty years; in other words, the dancing days of
Juliet's father ended some sixteen years before she was
born. Then follows the impassioned speech of Romeo, who
in the double contrast represents Youth and Love; he has
caught sight of Juliet, and his heart is lost. At once Tybalt
speaks, the pursuing Hate—

> This, by his voice, should be a Montague.
> Fetch me my rapier, boy.

COURTESY VERSUS VULGARITY

The inhospitality of environment has the effect of setting
Romeo and Juliet off by themselves, in a kind of loneliness.
At first we meet them in their proper society, surrounded
with friends and relatives; but as the story proceeds they are
estranged from their world. It is this common estrangement
that makes them appeal to us as one character, as devoted to
a single tragic fate. In a world such as theirs, of which the
strongest principle is family pride, to become strange to
one's own people is disaster enough, whether or not other
sufferings follow. . . . They had each found a sharer of their
confidence in place of the disqualified parents, but the
course of the story robs each of this comfort also. Romeo's
adviser is Friar Laurence, who as ghostly father serves
partly to represent the church, but also, as a philosophical
dreamer, more particularly to set up a contrast with the impetuous and unconsidering lover. . . .

That Juliet should have confided in the nurse is natural,
since the nurse alone of the household loved her. It is perhaps too easy, in view of the old woman's short-comings, to
forget her affection for Juliet. When Capulet in his fury lays
his insulting curse on his daughter, only the nurse braves
him—

> God in heaven bless her!
> You are to blame, my lord, to rate her so.

Yet her loyalty is not single; however privileged, she is still
the servant and messenger of the house. She enters the love-
story with words less sinister but no less ominous than Tybalt's call for his sword. Juliet and Romeo have just met, and

their fate is sealed; 'Madam, your mother craves a word with you,' says the nurse. Between the mother and the daughter she would be loyal to the daughter, according to her lights, but the situation is too difficult. She has, moreover, a radical failing which in time destroys Juliet's confidence in her; she represents that third contrast which Shakspere's audience would feel more acutely perhaps than we do—she is too vulgar to understand love. She illustrates inversely, as it were, the troubadour doctrine . . . that love is identical with gentleness of heart. Her heart was warm but not gentle; the coarseness of its fibre is shown by the anecdotes she inflicts upon her mistress, and—most fatally—in the sort of advice she gives to Juliet. So long as that advice concerns Romeo, Juliet nobly misunderstands it, and takes the counsel of physical passion to be only a rude phrasing of her own pure desires; but when the nurse urges her to marry Paris, on the ground that a living husband is better than the dead or as good as dead, Juliet perceives that they talk different languages, and she confides in the nurse no more. . . .

EARLIER ILLUSIONS OF LOVE

These contrasts between love and hate, youth and age, gentleness and vulgarity, which serve to remove Romeo and Juliet from their environment, Shakspere found almost ready in his material; he had but to clarify and emphasize them. But by rearranging certain episodes in the older story, he managed to isolate the lovers further, in a more subtle way—he cut them off from their own past, as he had estranged them from their surroundings, and by so doing he increased the feeling that a single experience, a single moment of fate, draws them together. Each had had in some sense an earlier love affair. Romeo had been infatuated with Rosaline, the pale lady with the dark eyes. If men fall in love first with love itself, and afterwards with a woman, the desire for Rosaline was but the illusion of an immature heart. . . . But Rosaline, though unseen, is far from an imaginary person. Her influence is perceptible, and in many unexpected ways she lights up Romeo's character for us. For example, she was related to the Capulets—she was a cousin of Juliet's. Was Romeo predisposed by his romantic temperament to fall in love with one of the hostile house? . . .

It is easy for the reader to think kindly of Rosaline, whom Romeo forgot, but hard not to bear some ill-will to Paris, whose wooing of Juliet precipitated the tragedy. Our interest in the fortunes of the newly wedded lovers makes us forget that Paris was no interloper. In the earlier versions he did present himself after the marriage and the separation of the lovers, but Shakspere makes him ask for Juliet's hand and receive the promise of it before Juliet had ever seen Romeo. The fact that he sought Capulet's permission as a preliminary to wooing the girl, does not indicate that he was less ardent than Romeo; had it not been for the feud, Romeo might well have followed the same course. Paris certainly appears to lack his rival's capacity for expression; we expect no torrent of ecstasy or of grief from his lips. Yet if reticence has been observed in Romeo as one of the maturing effects of true love, surely Paris deserves credit for the virtue from the first. His secret visit to Juliet's tomb shows that he was not devoid of sentiment. Indeed, it is singular that our pity should go out to Romeo and Juliet, and not to Paris, for he was in the truest sense a victim of love. . . .

PURITY OF CHARACTER AND CONDUCT

The feelings the play inspires in us indicate the innocence into which Shakspere transposed the story, and it is probably this innocence of feeling, more than the simplification of the plot, which made the play universal. The changes in the plot are important chiefly because they bring out new lights, new values, in the portrait of hero and heroine. In Brooke's poem Juliet was sophisticated, a 'wily wench,' who knew how to deceive her mother, and who after her marriage and Romeo's banishment encouraged Paris to make love to her. Her mother trusted neither her nor the nurse, but set another servant to watch them. In Brooke, Juliet is experienced and calculating; she knows all the symptoms of falling in love, so that she can diagnose her case, and provides herself with a reason for marrying Romeo if he can be got to propose—the hope that their union may end the feud. Shakspere assigns this good wish to the Friar, and takes from Juliet her craft and her experience, so that she becomes innocent and pure, almost fragile:

> So light a foot
> Will ne'er wear out the everlasting flint.

By betrothing her to Paris before she has even met Romeo, at a stroke the poet refines her character and converts Paris into a tragic victim. Shakspere also reduces her age, as we saw, from sixteen years to fourteen, just as a previous version reduced it to fourteen from sixteen; to increase the pathos by making her younger was perhaps a natural tendency. In Brooke's poem and in other accounts of the story, Romeo too was less fine. He went to the Capulet feast, for example, not in defiance of his friend's advice to fall in love with another beauty, but actually in the hope of finding a substitute for his obdurate mistress; Shakspere made him an uncalculating lover, with delicacy of speech and manners. ... He also brought out, as we saw, the contrast between the age of the parents and the youth of the lovers; he brought out the contrast of the Friar's philosophy with Romeo's passion, of the nurse's vulgarity with Juliet's refinement; he gave the tone of destiny to the feud by introducing Tybalt early, at the moment when Romeo sees Juliet; he developed in Mercutio that gaiety which now reinforces in the story the atmosphere of youth, just as he increased the suddenness with which the lovers realized their passion, making them fall in love actually at first sight; and by crowding the action of the story into days instead of months, he set the whole tragedy in the abrupt, volcanic atmosphere of youthful romance.

These changes contribute to a wonderful purity of character and conduct—all the more wonderful since the play exhibits, along with its spiritual innocence, such a natural frankness towards the physical basis of love as a close study of the text makes even startling. ... This fact answers our original question, why 'Romeo and Juliet' should to-day enjoy an immortality so general wherever English poetry is known. The sense of the dignity of life and the sympathy with human wrongs, to which time has accustomed mankind, have brought as an inevitable corollary a certain lukewarmness toward all ancient love-legends save this. Meanness and trickery now obscure the beauty of Helen, of Cleopatra, of Iseult, of Guinevere, and of their lovers; to them we do not look for modern ideals of youth. ... Of all the tragedies dear to the Renaissance, this alone of Romeo and Juliet became thoroughly accommodated to English ideals, and in the process, fitted to express the dream that young love now has of itself everywhere.

The Forces Driving the Play's Main Characters

Edward Dowden

Edward Dowden (1843–1913) was an Irish critic and biographer whose widely acclaimed book *Shakespere: His Mind and Art* (1875) was the first major work in English to attempt a unified analysis of Shakespeare's entire body of work. The following essay, taken from this landmark study, explores the five main characters of *Romeo and Juliet*—the two title characters, Mercutio, the Nurse, and Friar Laurence—in each case trying to pinpoint the forces motivating their personalities and actions. The author makes the point, for instance, that in the course of the play Romeo's experiences with love and death cause him to mature quickly from a young man living largely in a dream world of ideal love to an adult facing the stark realities of life. In his analysis, Dowden, like many other commentators, sometimes compares Shakespeare's handling of a character or situation to that of his immediate source, Arthur Brooke (author of the 1562 poem *The Tragical History of Romeus and Juliet*).

The mid-July heat broods over the five tragic days of [Romeo and Juliet]. The mad blood is stirring in men's veins during these hot summer days. There is a thunderous feeling in the moral element. The summer was needed also that the nights and mornings might quickly meet. The nights are those luminous nights from which the daylight seems never wholly to depart, nights through which the warmth of day still hangs over the trees and flowers. . . .

Romeo is not the determiner of events in the play. He does not stand prominently forward, a single figure in the first scene . . . soliloquising about his own persons and his plans.

From "Atmosphere and Character in *Romeo & Juliet*," in *Shakespere: His Mind and Art* by Edward Dowden (London: Henry S. King, 1875).

The first scene of the play prepares a place for Romeo, it presents the moral environment of the hero, it exhibits the feud of the houses which determines the lovers' fate, although they for a brief space forget these grim realities in the rapture of their joy. The strife of the houses Capulet and Montague appears in this first scene in its trivial, ludicrous aspect; threatening, however, in a moment to become earnest and formidable. The serving-men Gregory and Samson biting thumbs at the serving-men Abraham and Balthasar,— this is the obverse of the tragic show. Turn to the other side [of the play] and what do we see? The dead bodies of young and beautiful human creatures, of Tybalt and Paris, of Juliet and Romeo, the bloody harvest of the strife. This first scene, half ludicrous, but wholly grave, was written not without a reference to the final scene. The bandying of vulgar wit between the servants must not hide from us a certain grim irony which underlies the opening of the play. Here the two old rivals meet; they will meet again. And the prince appears in the last scene as in the first. Then old Capulet and Montague will be pacified; then they will consent to let their desolated lives decline to the grave in quietness. Meanwhile serving-men with a sense of personal dignity must bite their thumbs, and other incidents may happen.

ROMEO LOVE-BEWILDERED

Few critics of the play have omitted to call attention to the fact that Shakspere represents Romeo as already in love before he gives his heart to Juliet, in love with the pale-cheeked, dark-eyed, disdainful Rosaline. "If we are right," [eighteenth-century literary critic and poet Samuel Taylor] Coleridge wrote, ". . . in pronouncing this one of Shakspere's early dramas, it affords a strong instance of the fineness of his insight into the nature of the passions, that Romeo is introduced already love-bewildered." The circumstance is not of Shakspere's invention. He has retained it from Brooke's poem; but that he thought fit to retain the circumstance, fearlessly declaring that Romeo's supreme love is not his first love, is noteworthy. The contrast in the mind of the earlier poet between Rosaline, who

> From her youth was fostered evermore
> With vertues foode, and taught in schole, of wisdomes skil-
> full lore,

and Juliet, who yields to her passion, and by it is destroyed, was a contrast which Shakspere rejected as a piece of formal and barren morality. Of what character is the love of Romeo for Rosaline? . . . To him emotion which enriches and exalts itself with the imagination, emotion apart from thought, and apart from action, is an end in itself. Therefore it delights him to hover over his own sentiment, to brood upon it, to feed upon it richly. Romeo must needs steep his whole nature in feeling, and, if Juliet does not appear, he must love Rosaline.

Nevertheless the love of Rosaline cannot be to Romeo as is the love of Juliet. It is a law in moral dynamics, too little recognised, that the breadth, and height, and permanence of a feeling depend in a certain degree at least upon the actual force of its external cause. No ardour of self-protection, no abandonment prepense, no self-sustained energy, can create and shape a passion of equal volume, and possessing a like certainty and directness of advance with a passion shaped, determined, and for ever re-invigorated by positive, objective fact. Shakspere had become assured that the facts of the world are worthy to command our highest ardour, our most resolute action, our most solemn awe; and that the more we penetrate into fact the more will our nature be quickened, enriched, and exalted. The play of Romeo and Juliet exhibits to us the deliverance of a man from dream into reality. In Romeo's love of Rosaline we find represented the dream-life as yet undisturbed, the abandonment to emotion for emotion's sake. Romeo nurses his love; he sheds tears; he cultivates solitude; he utters his groans in the hearing of the comfortable friar. . . .

JULIET'S PASSION

He broods upon the luxury of his sorrow. And then Romeo meets Juliet. Juliet is an actual force beyond and above himself, a veritable fact of the world. Nevertheless there remains a certain clinging self-consciousness, an absence of perfect simplicity and directness even in Romeo's very real love of Juliet. This is placed by Shakspere in designed contrast with the singleness of Juliet's nature, her direct unerroneous passion which goes straight to its object, and never broods upon itself. It is Romeo who says in the garden scene,—

> How silver-sweet sound lovers' tongues by night,
> Like softest music to attending ears.

He has overheard the voice of Juliet, and he cannot answer her call until he has drained the sweetness of the sound. He is one of those men to whom the emotional atmosphere which is given out by the real object, and which surrounds it like a luminous mist, is more important than the reality itself. As he turns slowly away, loath to leave, Romeo exclaims,—

> Love goes toward love, as school-boys from their books,
> But love from love, towards school with heavy looks.

But Juliet's first thought is of the danger to which Romeo is exposed in her father's grounds. It is Juliet who will not allow the utterance of any oath because the whole reality of that night's event, terrible in its joy, has flashed upon her, and she, who lives in no golden haze of luxurious feeling, is aroused and alarmed by the sudden shock of too much happiness. It is Juliet who uses direct and simple words—

> Farewell compliment!
> Dost thou love me? I know thou wilt say "Ay,"
> And I will take thy word.

She has declared that her bounty is measureless, that her love is infinite, when a sudden prosaic interruption occurs; the nurse calls within, Juliet leaves the window, and Romeo is left alone. Is this new joy a dream?

> O blessed, blessed night! I am afeard,
> Being in night, all this is but a dream,
> Too flattering-sweet to be substantial.

But Juliet hastily reappears with words upon her lips which make it evident that it is no dream of joy in which she lives.

> Three words, dear Romeo, and good night indeed.
> If that thy bent of love be honourable,
> Thy purpose marriage, send me word to-morrow,
> By one that I'll procure to come to thee,
> Where, and what time thou wilt perform the rite,
> And all my fortunes at thy foot I'll lay,
> And follow thee, my lord, throughout the world.

The wholeness and crystalline purity of Juliet's passion is flawed by no double self. She is all and entire in each act of her soul. While Romeo, on the contrary, is as yet but half delivered from self-consciousness. . . .

A HIGH-STRUNG FORTITUDE

Juliet at once takes the lead. It is she who proposes and urges on the sudden marriage. She is impatient for complete self-surrender, eager that the deed should become perfect and irreversible. When, after the death of Tybalt, Romeo learns from the lips of the Friar that he has been condemned to banishment he is utterly unmanned. He abandons himself to helpless and hopeless despair. He turns the tender emotion upon himself, and extracts all the misery which is contained in that one word "banished." He throws himself upon the ground and grovels pitifully in the abjectness of his dismay. His will is unable to deal with his own emotions so as to subdue or control them. Upon the next day, after her casting away of her own kindred, after her parting with her husband, Juliet comes to the same cell of Friar Laurence, her face pale and traces of tears upon it which she cannot hide. Paris, the lover whom her father and mother have designed for Juliet, is there. She meets him with gay words, gallantly concealing the heart which is eager and trembling, and upheld from desperation only by a high-strung fortitude. Then when the door is shut her heart relieves itself, and she urges

ROMEO LEARNS OF HIS BANISHMENT

In this excerpt from act 3, scene 3, Friar Laurence informs Romeo that the Prince has banished him; the young man's emotional outburst exposes his still childish inability to deal with adult realities.

ROM. Father, what news? What is the Prince's doom?
What sorrow craves acquaintance at my hand
That I yet know not?
    FRIAR.   Too familiar
Is my dear son with such sour company.
I bring thee tidings of the Prince's doom.
    ROM. What less than doomsday is the Prince's doom?
    FRIAR. A gentler judgment vanished from his lips—
Not body's death, but body's banishment.
    ROM. Ha, banishment? Be merciful, say "death";
For exile hath more terror in his look,
Much more than death. Do not say "banishment."
    FRIAR. Hence from Verona art thou banished.
Be patient, for the world is broad and wide.
    ROM. There is no world without Verona walls,
But purgatory, torture, hell itself.
Hence banished is banisht from the world,
And world's exile is death. Then "banishment"
Is death mistermed. Calling death "banishment,"
Thou cuttst my head off with a golden axe
And smilest upon the stroke that murders me.
    FRIAR. O deadly sin! O rude unthankfulness!

the Friar, with passionate energy, to devise forthwith a remedy for the evil that has befallen.

In her home Juliet is now without adviser or sustainer; a girl of fourteen years, she stands the centre of a circle of power which is tyrannous, and pledged to crush her resistance; old Capulet (the Capulets are a fiery self-willed race, unlike the milder Montagues) has vehemently urged upon her the marriage with Count Paris. . . .

She turns to her mother,—the proud Italian matron, still young, who had not married for love, whose hatred is cold and deadly, and whose relation with the child, who is dear to her, is pathetically imperfect.

> Is there no pity sitting in the clouds,
> That sees into the bottom of my grief?
> O sweet my mother, cast me not away!

Thy fault our law calls death; but the kind Prince,
Taking thy part, hath rushed aside the law,
And turned that black word death to banishment.
This is dear mercy, and thou seest it not.
   ROM. 'Tis torture, and not mercy. Heaven is here,
Where Juliet lives; and every cat and dog
And little mouse, every unworthy thing,
Live here in heaven and may look on her;
But Romeo may not. More validity,
More honorable state, more courtship lives
In carrion flies than Romeo. They may seize
On the white wonder of dear Juliet's hand
And steal immortal blessing from her lips,
Who, even in pure and vestal modesty,
Still blush, as thinking their own kisses sin;
But Romeo may not—he is banished.
This may flies do, when I from this must fly;
They are free men, but I am banished.
And sayst thou yet that exile is not death?
Hadst thou no poison mixed, no sharp-ground knife,
No sudden mean of death, though ne'er so mean,
But "banished" to kill me—"banished"?
O friar, the damned use that word in hell;
Howling attends it! How hast thou the heart,
Being a divine, a ghostly confessor,
A sin-absolver, and my friend professed,
To mangle me with that word "banished"?

Delay this marriage for a month, a week.

Last she looks for support to her Nurse, turning in that dreadful moment with the instinct of childhood to the woman on whose breast she had lain, and uttering words of desperate and simple earnestness:—

O God! O nurse! how shall this be prevented?
.   .   .   .
Some comfort, nurse.

The same unfaltering severity with which a surgeon operates is shown by Shakspere in his fidelity here to the nurse's character. The gross and wanton heart, while the sun of prosperity is full, blossoms into broad vulgarity; and the raillery of Mercutio deals with it sufficiently. Now in the hour of trial her grossness rises to the dignity of a crime. "The Count is a lovely gentleman; Romeo's a dishclout to him; the second match excels the first; or if it does not, Juliet's first is dead, or as good as dead, being away from her.". . .

The Friar has given Juliet a phial containing a strange, untried mixture, and she is alone in her chamber. . . . In the night and the solitude, with a desperate deed to do, her imagination is intensely and morbidly excited. All the hideous secrets of the tomb appear before her. Suddenly in her disordered vision the figure of the murdered Tybalt rises, and is manifestly in pursuit of some one. Of whom? Not of Juliet, but of her lover who had slain him. A moment before Juliet had shrunk with horror from the thought of confronting Tybalt in the vault of the Capulets. But now Romeo is in danger. All fear deserts her. To stand by Romeo's side is her one necessity. With a confused sense that this draught will somehow place her close to the murderous Tybalt, and close to Romeo whom she would save, calling aloud to Tybalt to delay one moment,—"Stay, Tybalt, stay!"—she drains the phial, not "in a fit of fright," but with the words "Romeo! I come; this do I drink to thee."

MERCUTIO'S CARELESS COURAGE

The brooding nature of Romeo, which cherishes emotion, and lives in it, is made salient by contrast with Mercutio, who is all wit, and intellect, and vivacity, an uncontrollable play of gleaming and glancing life. Upon the morning after the betrothal with Juliet, a meeting happens between Romeo and Mercutio. Previously, while lover of Rosaline, Romeo had cultivated a lover-like melancholy. But now, partly because his blood runs gladly, partly because the union of soul with

Juliet has made the whole world more real and substantial, and things have grown too solid and lasting to be disturbed by a laugh, Romeo can contend in jest with Mercutio himself. . . . Mercutio and the nurse are Shakspere's creations in this play. For the character of the former he had but a slight hint in the poem of Arthur Brooke. There we read of Mercutio as a courtier who was bold among the bashful maidens as a lion among lambs, and we are told that he had an "ice-cold hand." Putting together these two suggestions, discovering a significance in them, and animating them with the breath of his own life, Shakspere created the brilliant figure which lights up the first half of Romeo and Juliet, and disappears when the colours become all too grave and sombre.

Romeo has accepted the great bond of love. Mercutio, with his ice-cold hand, the lion among maidens, chooses above all things a defiant liberty, a liberty of speech, gaily at war with the proprieties, an airy freedom of fancy, a careless and masterful courage in dealing with life, as though it were a matter of slight importance. He will not attach himself to either of the houses. He is invited by Capulet to the banquet; but he goes to the banquet in company with Romeo and the Montagues. He can do generous and disinterested things; but he will not submit to the trammels of being recognised as generous. He dies maintaining his freedom, and defying death with a jest. To be made worm's meat of so stupidly, by a villain that fights by the book of arithmetic, and through Romeo's awkwardness, is enough to make a man impatient. "A plague o' both your houses!" The death of Mercutio is like the removal of a shifting breadth of sunlight, which sparkles on the sea; now the clouds close in upon one another, and the stress of the gale begins.

ROMEO BECOMES A MAN

The moment that Romeo receives the false tidings of Juliet's death, is the moment of his assuming full manhood. Now, for the first time, he is completely delivered from the life of dream, completely adult, and able to act with an initiative in his own will, and with manly determination. Accordingly, he now speaks with masculine directness and energy:—

Is it even so? Then I defy you, stars!

Yes; he is now master of events; the stars cannot alter his course. . . .

These words because they are the simplest are amongst
the most memorable that Romeo utters. Is this indeed the
same Romeo who sighed, and wept, and spoke sonnet-wise,
and penned himself in his chamber, shutting the daylight
out for love of Rosaline? Now passion, imagination, and will,
are fused together, and Romeo who was weak has at length
become strong.

In two noteworthy particulars Shakspere has varied from
his original. He has compressed the action from some
months into four or five days. Thus precipitancy is added to
the course of events and passions. Shakspere has also made
the catastrophe more calamitous than it is in Brooke's poem.
It was his invention to bring Paris across Romeo in the
church-yard. Paris comes to strew his flowers, uttering in a
rhymed sextain (such as might have fallen from Romeo's
lips in the first Act), his pretty lamentation. Romeo goes res-
olutely forward to death. He is no longer "young Romeo,"
but adult, and Paris is the boy. He speaks with the gentleness, and with the authority of one who knows what life and
death are, of one who has gained the superior position of
those who are about to die over those who still may live:

> Good, gentle youth, tempt not a desperate man.
> Fly hence and leave me; think upon these gone;
> Let them affright thee. I beseech thee, youth,
> Put not another sin upon my head,
> By urging me to fury. . . .

Friar Laurence remains to furnish the Prince with an explanation of the events. It is impossible to agree with those
critics . . . who represent the Friar as a kind of chorus ex-
pressing Shakspere's own ethical ideas, and his opinions re-
specting the characters and action. It is not Shakspere's practice to expound the moralities of his artistic creations; nor
does he ever by means of a chorus stand above and outside
the men and women of his plays, who are bone of his bone
and flesh of his flesh. . . . Friar Laurence also is moving in
the cloud, and misled by error as well as the rest. Shakspere
has never made the moderate, self-possessed, sedate person,
a final or absolute judge of the impulsive and the passionate;
the one sees a side of truth which is unseen by the other; but
to neither is the whole truth visible. The Friar had supposed
that by virtue of his prudence, his moderation, his sage
counsels, his amiable sophistries, he could guide these two
young, passionate lives, and do away the old tradition of en-

mity between the houses. There in the tomb of the Capulets is the return brought in by his investment of kindly scheming. Shakspere did not believe that the highest wisdom of human life was acquirable by mild, monastic meditation, and by gathering of simples in the coolness of the dawn. Friar Laurence too, old man, has his lesson to learn. . . .

FROM THE HORROR OF THE TOMB TO A BETTER LIFE

Shakspere did not intend that the feeling evoked by the last scene of this tragedy of Romeo and Juliet should be one of hopeless sorrow or despair in presence of failure, ruin, and miserable collapse. Juliet and Romeo, to whom Verona has been a harsh step-mother, have accomplished their lives. They loved perfectly. Romeo had attained to manhood. Juliet had suddenly blossomed into heroic womanhood. Through her, and through anguish and joy, her lover had emerged from the life of dream into the waking life of truth. Juliet had saved his soul; she had rescued him from abandonment to spurious feeling, from abandonment to morbid self-consciousness, and the enervating luxury of emotion for emotion's sake. What more was needed? And as secondary to all this, the enmity of the houses is appeased. Montague will raise in pure gold the statue of true and faithful Juliet; Capulet will place Romeo by her side. Their lives are accomplished; they go to take up their place in the large history of the world, which contains many such things. Shakspere in this last scene carries forward our imagination from the horror of the tomb to the better life of man, when such love as that of Juliet and Romeo will be publicly honoured, and remembered by a memorial all gold.

The Characters' Impulsiveness Is the Villain of the Play

Bert Cardullo

Most of Shakespeare's tragedies have one or more villains who cause or at least complicate the troubles of the main characters. In *Othello*, for example, the title character's assistant, Iago, creates havoc by falsely claiming that Othello's wife is unfaithful. Occasionally, the main character is the villain, as in the case of the murderous title character in *Richard III*. By contrast, *Romeo and Juliet* arguably has no clearcut villain. Many scholars have suggested that Shakespeare instead relied on chance, unfortunate accidents, and so on to bring about the lovers' tragic circumstances, and that this is the main weakness of the play. In this essay, Bert Cardullo, a noted drama critic and professor at the University of Michigan in Ann Arbor, argues that it is not chance but character that drives the play's tragic workings; specifically, he says, it is the consistently impulsive behavior of several of the main characters that leads to fatal mistakes and bloodshed. Cardullo especially singles out the numerous rash acts of Friar Laurence, who ironically admonishes Romeo to act "wisely and slow" and then proceeds to do the opposite himself.

"It has been objected," writes [Shakespearean scholar] Frank Kermode, "that *[Romeo and Juliet]* lacks tragic necessity—that the story becomes tragic only by a trick. . . . [There is a conviction that] Shakespeare offends against his own criteria for tragedy by allowing mere chance to determine the destiny of the hero and heroine." We learn of the "trick" when Friar John, whom Friar Laurence has sent to Mantua with a letter telling Romeo to come and take Juliet away

From "The Friar's Flaw, the Play's Tragedy: The Experiment of *Romeo and Juliet*" by Bert Cardullo, *CLA Journal*, vol. 28, no. 4, June 1985. Reprinted by permission of the College Language Association.

when she awakens from her long sleep, returns. . . . The trick, supposedly, is the plague that has afflicted Verona and delayed Friar John, because he just happened to choose for a traveling companion a brother who had been attending the ill. [Scholar] R.G. Moulton is one of those who argue that "the . . . tragedy has all been brought about by [chance, by the] accidental detention of Friar John." Brian Gibbons [another noted literary scholar] argues similarly of Romeo's discovery that a feast is to take place at Capulet's house: "[Here] Shakespeare emphasizes the element of chance in the action. The servant Capulet has chosen [to deliver invitations] happens to be illiterate, a fact which his master has forgotten. . . . The meeting with Romeo is sheer accident and after the servant turns away, by chance Romeo regrets his off-hand answer and takes the list."

Character, not chance, is at work at this point in the play. Capulet, in his typically rash manner, sends an illiterate servant on an errand that requires reading. The servant's meeting with Romeo may be an accident, but Shakespeare undercuts this aspect of it and emphasizes Romeo's own impulsiveness. He teases the servant, claiming to be able to read "if I know the letters and the language"—the servant interprets this to mean that Romeo cannot read, when it really means that he can read only the language he knows. When the servant starts on his way to find someone who can read, Romeo suddenly decides to help him and calls him back; he reads the list aloud and learns that the people on it are invited to Capulet's house. Capulet repeats this pattern in Act III, Scene iv: Paris starts to leave and he impulsively calls him back, offering him Juliet's hand. Friar Laurence repeats it again in Act IV, Scene i. After telling Juliet that nothing can postpone her marriage to Paris and hearing her declare that she will kill herself rather than break her vow to Romeo, he says, "Hold, daughter," echoing Romeo's "Stay, fellow" to the servant, and on the spur of the moment offers her, in the sleeping potion, a desperate way out of her dilemma.

Romeo's and Capulet's impulsiveness or rashness has been well documented. Capulet's offer of Juliet in marriage to Paris without first consulting his daughter is followed by the equally impulsive, and ultimately disastrous, action of advancing the wedding from Thursday to Wednesday. The most obvious example of impulsive behavior on Romeo's part occurs when, upon hearing from Balthasar that Juliet is dead, he goes immediately to the Apothecary's to buy poison with which to kill himself at her side, instead of first investigating the circumstances of her "death." Unlike Romeo's and Capulet's, Friar Laurence's rashness has not been explored; it is, however, essential to an understanding of the play as tragic as opposed to pathetic.

THE FRIAR'S RASHNESS

Just as the illiterate servant, Paris, and Juliet in the above examples are not offered what they desire by chance, neither is Friar John detained by the plague by chance. The first cause of his delay is Friar Laurence's rashness. He sends John to Mantua alone, when he should remember, as Brian Gibbons points out, that "the rule of the [Franciscan] order forbade [Friar John] to travel without the company of another [Franciscan] friar." John is detained because the companion that he finds has had contact with the sick; as a precaution, both he and the other friar are quarantined to prevent the spread of the disease. Even if it is argued that it was Friar John's responsibility to find a traveling companion, not Friar Laurence's to find one for him, the latter should still have foreseen the improbability of his confrere's choosing a "safe" Franciscan companion in a city beset by the plague (the Franciscans would be ministering to the sick, and would therefore be capable of spreading the infection). He should have gone to the trouble of providing a Franciscan companion for Friar John who had not had contact with the disease, or perhaps he should even have gone with him himself. Surely Friar Laurence knew of the plague's existence in Verona. Had Friar John left the city immediately in the company of a "safe" member of his order, he would never have been delayed and would have been able to deliver the letter to Romeo. . . .

In my view, the flaw of impulsiveness or rashness does explain the tragedy of *Romeo and Juliet*. Friar Laurence's rashness is responsible for Friar John's detention, not chance. And it is equally responsible for Balthasar's reaching Mantua, undeterred, with news of Juliet's "death." It is the Friar's fault that Balthasar is unaware of her feigned death. In Act III, upon sending Romeo to spend the night with Juliet and then to flee to Mantua, Friar Laurence says to him, "I'll find out your man, / And he shall signify from time to time / Every good hap to you that chances here." We know that, before departing for Mantua, Romeo tells Balthasar of his role as happy go-between, since the latter says to him in Act V, "O pardon me for bringing these ill news, / Since you did leave it for my office, sir." It is another mark of Romeo's impulsiveness that he does not question this *"ill* news" from a source whose office it was to "signify from time to time / Every *good* hap to [him] that chances [in Verona]." Romeo asks if Balthasar has been sent by the Friar, but he gets no reply and neglects to ask again. He never inquires what his servant or Friar Laurence knows about the circumstances surrounding the death of one so young as Juliet.

THEY STUMBLE THAT RUN FAST

The Friar, of course, never does find Balthasar and apprise him of the plan to get Juliet out of the marriage to Paris so that she can be reunited with Romeo. Had he sent *Balthasar* instead of Friar John to Mantua with the letter, the deaths of Romeo and Juliet would have been prevented. Presumably, Romeo would have returned to Verona at the appointed time to take Juliet away. Just as, in his haste to aid Romeo and Juliet, Friar Laurence forgets about the infectious disease that afflicts Verona and that will ultimately detain Friar John, he forgets to send Balthasar in John's place (as he had told Romeo he would) and even to inform him of the plan to reunite the lovers. Friar Laurence and Balthasar are acting independently to serve Romeo, whereas they should be acting together. Similarly, Friar John is acting "independently" when he leaves Friar Laurence's cell without a Franciscan companion. The image of John and a fellow friar, finally acting together but quarantined for it, and helpless to prevent the tragedy, is the opposite of that of Friar Laurence and Balthasar at the end of the play, finally discovering each other's separate actions but "freed" or pardoned for them by the Prince, and able to join in the two families' reconciliation.

The most obvious example of Friar Laurence's rashness or impulsiveness occurs in Act II, when he decides to honor Romeo's request to marry Juliet. The Friar's intentions are good; he hopes, by joining the lovers in marriage, "to turn [their] households' rancour to pure love." But he acts without considering fully the possible consequences of such a secret marriage between members of feuding families. Ironically, he violates his own dictum: "Wisely and slow; they stumble that run fast." In order to make Friar Laurence's

THE NURSE TURNS ON ROMEO

In this excerpt from act 3, scene 5, Juliet, having learned of Romeo's banishment, turns to her nurse for comfort, only to hear the woman, in her own display of impulsive behavior, disparage him in favor of Lord Capulet's choice, young Paris.

JUL. O God!—O nurse, how shall this be prevented?
My husband is on earth, my faith in heaven.
How shall that faith return again to earth
Unless that husband send it me from heaven
By leaving earth? Comfort me, counsel me.
Alack, alack, that heaven should practice stratagems
Upon so soft a subject as myself!
What sayst thou? Hast thou not a word of joy?
Some comfort, nurse.
    NURSE.   Faith, here it is.
Romeo is banisht; and all the world to nothing
That he dares ne'er come back to challenge you;
Or if he do, it needs must be by stealth.
Then, since the case so stands as now it doth,
I think it best you married with the County.
O, he's a lovely gentleman!
Romeo's a dishclout to him. An eagle, madam,
Hath not so green, so quick, so fair an eye
As Paris hath. Beshrew my very heart,
I think you are happy in this second match,
For it excels your first; or if it did not,
Your first is dead—or 'twere as good he were
As living here and you no use of him.
    JUL. Speakst thou this from thy heart?
    NURSE. And from my soul too; else beshrew them both.
    JUL. Amen!
    NURSE. What?
    JUL. Well, thou hast comforted me marvelous much.
Go in; and tell my lady I am gone,
Having displeased my father, to Laurence' cell,
To make confession and to be absolved.
    NURSE. Marry, I will; and this is wisely done.
    JUL. Ancient damnation! O most wicked fiend!
Is it more sin to wish me thus forsworn,
Or to dispraise my lord with that same tongue
Which she hath praised him with above compare
So many thousand times? Go, counselor!
Thou and my bosom henceforth shall be twain.
I'll to the friar to know his remedy.
If all else fail, myself have power to die.

rashness stand out, Shakespeare contrasts it with the hesitation or delay of the Nurse—the only other character (except perhaps Balthasar) with knowledge of Romeo and Juliet's secret union, and one who exhibits her own bit of impulsiveness in switching her preference of husbands for Juliet from Romeo to Paris once the former has been banished from Verona. Like the other characters' impulsiveness, the Nurse's turns out to have tragic consequences: her sudden disparagement of Romeo is the immediate cause of Juliet's decision to ask the Friar how she can remain faithful to him, how she can avoid marriage to Paris. . . .

A SPIRITUAL PLAGUE

Character, then—Friar Laurence's, Capulet's, Romeo's—determines the destiny of Romeo and Juliet, not chance. It has often been said that the play is in part about the hastiness of youth. I would say that it is in part about the hastiness of everyone, of the old as well as the young. One of the oddities of this tragedy is that the flaw of impulsiveness or rashness is shared by at least three characters (Juliet's and the Nurse's impulsive moments are not as numerous and significant as the three men's. Clearly Tybalt and Mercutio are impulsive, though not as central to the action as the trio; the impulsiveness of Capulet extends all the way to his servants, who start the fight with Montague's men in the first scene.)

Another oddity is that neither Capulet, Romeo, nor Friar Laurence ever has any recognition of his flaw. This suggests, less that they are not fully tragic or sufficiently introspective, than that their impulsiveness was bred by the unnatural state in which they lived—by the long-standing feud between the two families, which affected even non-family members like Friar Laurence. This may help to explain Shakespeare's curious mention only one time of the "infectious pestilence" afflicting Verona. The infectious pestilence may be seen as a metaphor for the spiritual one—the feud and its resultant impulsiveness—bedeviling two prominent families in the city and their circles. Friar John is confined so as to prevent the spread of infection and kill the plague. His confinement leads to the deaths of Romeo and Juliet and as a result, paradoxically, to the killing of the spiritual plague afflicting their families.

Once the feud is about to end as a consequence of the deaths of the lovers, impulsiveness in characters like Capulet and Friar Laurence disappears; tranquility rules in its place. Impulsiveness nearly possesses a life of its own in *Romeo and Juliet;* to the extent that no one mentions the original cause of the feud, the flaw that it bred appears almost as one disconnected from character. It comes to Verona, one does not know exactly whence, and it goes. Romeo gives the following speech before going to the feast at Capulet's house:

> I fear too early, for my mind misgives
> Some consequence yet hanging in the stars
> Shall bitterly begin his fearful date
> With this night's revels, and expire the term
> Of a despised life clos'd in my breast
> By some vile forfeit of untimely death.
> But he that hath the steerage of my course
> Direct my suit.

Perhaps the "despised life" enclosed in Romeo's breast is the very impulsiveness that I have been speaking of. And perhaps the "consequence yet hanging in the stars" is its destruction at its own hands. Impulsiveness has spread among the members of both families, and to their friends, to the point that it must conflict with itself: Romeo and Juliet's marriage, with Capulet's intention to give his daughter to Paris; Friar Laurence's plan to save Juliet from a second union, with Capulet's desire to see her wed even earlier than planned; Juliet's feigned death, with Romeo's suicide.

The Real Villain

Impulsiveness is the real villain in this play that has no villains. It finally extinguishes itself, but not before Mercutio, Tybalt, Paris, Romeo, and Juliet are killed by it. Obviously, we do not lament impulsiveness' passing at the end of *Romeo and Juliet.* But we may have been fascinated by its having afflicted almost everyone in the circumscribed world of the drama, instead of isolating itself in a single tragic figure. This may have something to do with the play's origins in comedy. The reconciliation of two feuding houses through marriage is normally a subject of comedy; Shakespeare made it a subject of tragedy. . . . Accordingly the thought and the talk at the end of *Romeo and Juliet* are of reconciliation of the Montague and Capulet families, not of full tragic recognition; no one identifies the flaw that led to the catastrophe, or any individual manifestations of it (Friar Laurence admits that he married Romeo and Juliet and gave her the sleeping potion, but he does not connect these actions with impulsiveness or rashness, leaving it to the Prince to decide if he has done anything wrong). Shakespeare has his "comic" ending, arrived at by a tragic route.

Clearly Shakespeare's other tragedies contain comedy, but none joins comedy to tragedy in the special way that *Romeo and Juliet* does. [Scholar] Lawrence Edward Bowling has written:

> In its broadest terms, *Romeo and Juliet* deals with the wholeness and complexity of things, in contrast with a partial and simple view. . . . The most important embodiment of the general theme deals with the discovery on the part of Romeo and Juliet and members of their families that individual human beings are not composed of abstract good or evil—that humanity is composed not of villains and saints but of human beings more or less alike. . . . The meaning and significance of *Romeo and Juliet* may be more completely understood if we see the play as part of [the] greater movement toward a more relative and flexible view of human nature and human conduct.

The meaning and significance of *Romeo and Juliet* may be more completely understood if we also regard its tragic treatment of a traditionally comic subject as part of the greater movement toward seeing things in their wholeness and complexity, instead of from a partial and simple point of view—seeing people and events neither as exclusively comic nor exclusively tragic, but as a combination of the two.

The Masquerade Is the Play's Central Reference Point

Kathleen McLuskie

This insightful essay by Kathleen McLuskie of the University of Southampton in England, examines Shakespeare's ambitious use of the masque as a unifying element for the characters and plot of *Romeo and Juliet*. Here, the term *masque* has two meanings. First, as was the case in Renaissance and Elizabethan times, it denotes a lavish party or theatrical event; and in the play, Lord Capulet throws a masqued (masked) ball that Romeo and his friends attend, of course, wearing masks. The more specific meaning of masque is the idea of a masquerade itself, that is, the act of concealing one's identity by the use of a mask. According to McLuskie, Shakespeare used this image not only as a convenient way of getting Romeo and his friends into the party, but also as a symbol, throughout the course of the play, of people masking and then unmasking their feelings; of characters hiding and later revealing the truth.

Many of the commentators on *Romeo and Juliet* have suggested that the tragic outcome of the plot hinges merely on a series of coincidences in the time structure of the plot. Capulet hastens Juliet's marriage to Paris, Friar John arrives too late in Mantua and Juliet awakens just too late to prevent Romeo from suicide. Yet the play has far more force than simply a sad story of young lovers. The play is about 'the fearful passage of their death-marked love' and it arouses a feeling of tragic inevitability which runs throughout the plot and creates a suspense for which the tragic outcome is the only possible resolution. This feeling has to be aroused from the very beginning of the action and Shakespeare succeeds

From "Shakespeare's 'Earth-Treading Stars': The Image of the Masque in *Romeo and Juliet*" by Kathleen McLuskie, in *Shakespeare Survey*, vol. 24, edited by Kenneth Muir (Cambridge: Cambridge University Press, 1971); ©1971 by Kathleen McLuskie. Reprinted by permission of the author.

in this by presenting the meeting of the lovers in a masque. The masque solves perfectly the plot problem of how to get Romeo into the Capulet household but it also makes it into a theatrically significant event by the spectacular nature of the scene and the atmosphere which it creates. Romeo must enter the Capulet banquet as the herald of love and the masque evokes this atmosphere of youth and revelling. We see the associations of the masque for the characters involved when Capulet remembers

> the day
> That I have worn a visor and could tell
> A whispering tale in a fair lady's ear,
> Such as would please

He regards it as a game of love for youth and we remember that the great novelty and attraction of the masque was that it allowed masqued strangers to mingle with the guests. . . .

Romeo and Juliet are both going to the masque as lovers even before they have met. In the scene where the masque is first mentioned Benvolio persuades Romeo to go to the feast so that he may compare Rosaline with 'all the admired beauties of Verona'. He agrees to go 'to rejoice in splendour of mine own' and the magic of the masque enables him to find one even more splendid who will become his own in a way that Rosaline could never have been. In the following scene there is another reminder that the masque is a celebration of love for when Lady Capulet is talking to Juliet of her proposed marriage to Paris she says

> Can you love the gentleman?
> This night you shall behold him at our feast. . .

MORE SINISTER CONNOTATIONS

The masque, however, has other more sinister connotations since it allows hostile strangers entrance to another house with possibly dangerous consequences. . . . It is important that in the context of the Montague and Capulet feud Romeo is a potentially hostile stranger and in the midst of the revelling the reminder of the feud comes home to the audience in Tybalt's furious

> What, dares the slave
> Come hither, covered with an antic face,
> To fleer and scorn at our solemnity.

To Tybalt a masque can only be a temporary cover for the activities of the real world where names and families, the outward aspects of a man, are the reality for which he is prepared to violate all ceremony, and the ceremony of the masque insisted on by Capulet when he refuses to allow Tybalt to challenge Romeo is meaningless. To offset Tybalt's attitude we have the other various statements made about masking in the play. Romeo's first reference to masks talks of

> These happy masks that kiss fair ladies' brows,
> Being black, puts us in mind they hide the fair.

The mask is hiding something more beautiful than itself.

THE ELIZABETHAN MASQUE

In Romeo and Juliet, *Shakespeare in a sense staged a "masque within a masque," for, as scholar Charles J. Sisson here explains, the staging of the play was itself a masque.*

In the greatest days of the Elizabethan drama spectacle was in the main confined to such effects as can be obtained by splendour of costume, upon which the actors spared no expense, and which served to dress the stage to the admiration of the spectators. But with the reign of James came the vogue of the Court masque, which joined the dance and music with symbolic costume and also with increasingly elaborate scenic and architectural display, and machines, designed by such men as Inigo Jones, and carried out at enormous expense to the King. With this the King entertained his Court and himself, as well as foreign visitors whom it was desired to impress. Such displays had their inevitable repercussion on the professional stage, and could best be emulated in the 'private' houses, in enclosed rooms and by artificial light, before a more select audience. Shakespeare's later plays betray the influence of the masque and by their strong masque element show how he and his company catered for the new taste.

For Mercutio the mask is permanent and the visor which he puts on before the Capulet ball is simply an alternative to the mask of every day. He says

> Give me a case to put my visage in.
> A visor for a visor! What care I
> What curious eye cloth quote deformities?
> Here are the beetle brows shall blush for me.

In the context of the play a masque provides a suitable protective anonymity and creates a world where Romeo and Juliet can meet simply as a young man and a girl. This is made explicit in the scene after the banquet when Juliet, realising that Romeo has overheard her expression of love, says

> Thou knowest the mask of night is on my face,
> Else would a maiden blush bepaint my cheek . . .

From behind their masks the lovers can create a delightful world of holy palmers expressed in the perfect symmetry of the sonnet which is formed by their first greeting. Nevertheless the insecurity of this world is shown by placing immediately before the sonnet Tybalt's threatening reminder of the outside world

> I will withdraw; but this intrusion shall,
> Now seeming sweet, convert to bitt'rest gall.

Thus within the one scene of the masque we have all the elements of the story and its tragic outcome. The arrival of Romeo with masquers brings in the love affair which is the centre of the plot but it also enrages Tybalt against him, causing their later duel with all its tragic consequences of banishment and death. The image of the masque, moreover, is echoed in other situations throughout the play, referring back to the scene of the lovers' meeting and contrasting with the later tragic events.

THE GAME OF DUELLING

The first scene where the events of the tragedy begin to crowd in on the lovers is the death of Tybalt, and here again there is the echo of the masque in the challenging exchange:

> TYBALT. Mercutio, thou consortest with Romeo.

> MERCUTIO. Consort! What, dost thou make us minstrels? An thou make minstrels of us, look to hear nothing but discords. Here's my fiddlestick; here's that shall make you dance. Zounds, consort!

Mercutio is here being quarrelsome and simply playing with Tybalt's words but it is significant that his word-play should develop into the imagery of music and dancing associated with the masque. Tybalt is coming to settle the score for Romeo's intrusion into the Capulet feast and Mercutio's words are a reminder of how Tybalt did not take part in the dancing on that occasion. In the Franco Zeffirelli production [the 1968 film] of the play the fighting as well as the dancing was seen as just another activity of the lively youth of Verona. But just as Romeo and Juliet took the game of love in the masque seriously enough to get married, in this scene we see the game of duelling being played for high stakes and Romeo is plunged into the real world where he has to avenge a friend and then take the consequences of his action. Duelling can only be a game if all the participants are following the same rules, but just as Tybalt refused to play by the rules of the masque, the rules of hospitality and the convention of not recognising the masquers, here he breaks the convention of the duel and fatally wounds Mercutio under Romeo's arm.

THE LOVERS BECOME ADULTS

With the death of Tybalt the action moves on to a more mature level. The lovers have to be seen to be adults for the play to evoke tragedy rather than pathos. Romeo has become a man in first refusing to join in the spurious game of honour. He will not fight with Tybalt since he is now committed to the higher level of his love for Juliet. His later challenge to Tybalt is based on the reality of Mercutio's death and he then has to cope with the real consequences of a manly action.

Similarly in the scene where the nurse brings Juliet news of her cousin's death we see her movement to maturity in love which is based, not on the excitement of a masque and a moonlit encounter in an orchard, but on the commitment of her new role. Her immediate reaction to the news of Tybalt's death takes us back again to the masque for she feels, as Tybalt did on that occasion, that Romeo's was a 'serpent heart, hid with a flowering face'. Through the course of this scene, however, she comes to realise the narrowness of this division into serpents and flowers, Montague and Capulets. She realises that she must now stand with her husband in a world where the comfort is partial—

My husband lives that Tybalt would have slain
And Tybalt's dead that would have slain my husband.

In this world created by the death of Mercutio the masque is no sanctuary and the next time we hear the image of the masque it heralds not a joyful meeting but a sorrowful parting. When the lovers part at daybreak after their wedding night Juliet, seeing the dawn, insists

Yond light is not daylight; I know it, I:
It is some meteor that the sun exhales
To be to thee this night a torch-bearer,
And light thee on thy way to Mantua.

We have seen how the masque, throughout the plot, becomes a kind of double image containing the seeds of joy as well as tragedy and this feeling is reinforced by the ideas be-

hind the images which are used to talk about the masque
and the physical presence of the masquers. When Capulet
first mentions the banquet to Paris he says

> At my poor house look to behold this night
> Earth-treading stars that make dark heaven light.
> Such comfort as do lusty young men feel
> When well-apparell'd April on the heel
> Of limping winter treads, even such delight
> Among fresh female buds shall you this night
> Inherit at this house.

. . . The earth-treading stars are an echo of the 'solemne
feast' in *Hero end Leander* where

> resorted many a wandering guest
> To meet their loves; such as had none at all
> Came lovers home from this great festival
> For every street like to a firmament
> Glistered with breathing stars

This again associates the feast with the birth of love but it
also foreshadows the physical arrival of the masquers who,
with their torches, are the embodiment of light brought to
the banquet. They *are* the earth-treading stars and especially
Romeo who is not in fact a masquer but a torch-bearer. He
insisted to Benvolio

> Give me a torch; I am not for this ambling;
> Being but heavy, I will bear the light.
> Let wantons, light of heart,
> Tickle the senseless rushes with their heels . . .
> I'll be a candle-holder and look on

The choice of this image is important since it suggests the
image of a feast reflecting the harmony of the stars as well
as their light. The masquers will be earth-treading stars
since dancing was meant to reflect the harmonious movement of the heavens. . . . Dancing at its highest figures the
harmony of the spheres and we see in the masquing scene
Capulet's vain attempt to maintain this harmony at his feast
when he forbids Tybalt to challenge Romeo. Nevertheless,
we know then that the heavenly harmony of the lovers cannot survive in Verona. . . .

THE STARS, THE LOVERS, AND DEATH

The next time that the star image appears Juliet is talking of
death, although happily, within the context of her love for
Romeo:

> Come, gentle night, come, loving black-brow'd night,

> Give me my Romeo; and, when he shall die,
> Take him and cut him out in little stars,
> And he will make the face of heaven so fine
> That all the world will be in love with night,
> And pay no worship to the garish sun.

The lovers could be harmonious stars through their love but this could also be achieved through a death which would not deny their love. . . .

In the later part of the play Romeo and death are specifically related. The next feast that takes place is the preparation for Juliet's wedding and here death in the midst of feasting seems actually to be true. Capulet tells Paris

> the night before thy wedding day
> Hath Death lain with thy wife. There she lies,
> Flower as she was, deflowered by him.
> Death is my son-in-law, Death is my heir;
> My daughter he hath wedded.

The Death who had lain with Juliet was Romeo but since we know that she is in fact alive we see that he has only brought her death in the world of the Capulets. There is thus hope that the final death is also death of true love to the world outside and the road to immortality on a higher sphere. [Scholar] Warren Smith has pointed out that the rosemary which bestrews Juliet's corpse was used at weddings as well as funerals, for it is a symbol of rebirth and immortality. The funeral procession will take Juliet to her final wedding with Death who, as Capulet has said, is Romeo. Paris's lament over Juliet

> O love! O life!—not life, but love in death!

suggests the final fate of the lovers who die in love and through their love in order to attain the harmony of the stars which is impossible in the world of Verona.

Some Consequence, Yet Hanging in the Stars

The feeling of triumph is very strong in the graveyard scene and this is achieved by bringing in the theme and imagery of the first banquet. When Romeo goes to bury Paris in the Capulet vault he exclaims

> A grave? O no! A lantern, slaught'red youth;
> For here lies Juliet, and her beauty makes
> This vault a feasting presence full of light

'A feasting presence full of light' is surely a reference to the simply theatrical effect of the arrival of torch-bearers at a banquet and the image of light reminds us of Juliet as she was at that banquet. The first time he sees her Romeo says

> O, she doth teach the torches to burn bright!
> It seems she hangs upon the cheek of night
> As a rich jewel in an Ethiop's ear...

The echo of the banquet is a tragic recollection of their early love but where there is feasting there is the love of 'earth-treading stars' and in the grave Romeo believes that 'unsubstantial death is amorous'. He has come as Death to a different kind of banquet and he brings a different kind of death whereby

> Thou art not conquer'd; beauty's ensign yet
> Is crimson in thy lips and in thy cheeks,
> And death's pale flag is not advanced there.

But the triumph of the lovers in their death cannot hinge on the feeling of this scene alone, however important this is in the theatre. The feeling is created and backed up by the image of Romeo's dreams which goes through the play and is also associated with the masque. . . . The masque in *Romeo and Juliet is* placed in a context of premonitory dreams by the discussion of Romeo's dream when the masquers are preparing.

Romeo is worried about going to the masque because of his dream which has foreshadowed

> Some consequence, yet hanging in the stars,
> Shall bitterly begin his fearful date
> With this night's revels, and expire the term
> Of a despised life clos'd in my breast,
> By some vile forfeit of untimely death.

Mercutio rejects the possibility of significant dreams, for as far as he is concerned dreams are merely the result of direct sense impressions and an idle romanticising of the everyday world. . . . We would like to be able to agree with Mercutio when he is denying Romeo's fears, but we see how his attitude also makes it impossible to accept the dream of love, as we see when he jeers at Romeo after the masque and his scorn takes on the explicitly sexual note of

> If love be blind, love cannot hit the mark.
> Now will he sit under a medlar tree,
> And wish his mistress were that kind of fruit
> As maids call medlars when they laugh alone.

Mercutio rejects both the love and the tragedy but we see in the play that in the world of Verona it is impossible to have one without the other. . . .

THE DREAM OF LOVE

The image of the dream occupies the same kind of paradoxical position in the play as that of the masque. Romeo and Juliet's love is a dream and so it cannot exist in the world of sense and action occupied by Mercutio and the Nurse for whom one man is much the same as another. Yet if Romeo's premonitory dream is true, the dream of love is also true on a level beyond that of the world of Verona. The acceptance of both fulfilled love and tragedy allows the lovers to achieve a glory denied to the exponents of the world of sense.

The final scene, with its images of light and feasting, is also given a note of triumph by the final dream. Before Romeo hears of Juliet's death he has another dream:

> I dreamt my lady came and found me dead—
> Strange dream, that gives a dead man leave to think!—
> And breath'd such life with kisses in my lips
> That I reviv'd and was an emperor.

On one level this dream is poignantly ironic since it is Romeo who comes and finds Juliet dead and her last kisses are an attempt to kill herself with the poison from his lips. Nevertheless the premonition is not simply a reversal of what happens but foretells the events after Juliet has kissed Romeo. The dream of love does give a dead man leave to think, for their love makes their death part of the progress beyond the world of sense. The world of action can only provide the kind of death which comes to Mercutio who dies cursing, and in any case it is based on the much more false dreams of spurious honour and sexual prowess.

The masque in *Romeo and Juliet* provides an image of the brief moment of harmony in which it was possible for Romeo and Juliet to fall in love. It is presented theatrically in the stage picture of the 'feasting presence full of light' and poetically in the image of the earth-treading stars. This moment of harmony becomes a central point of reference for the whole play, and its controlling images of revelry within danger, sudden light in darkness, and a dream which transcends reality, are the opposites, contrasting and yet reconcilable, which make for the vitality of the play.

CHAPTER 2

Themes and Ideas Developed in *Romeo and Juliet*

READINGS ON
ROMEO AND JULIET

Echoes of *Romeo and Juliet* in *A Midsummer Night's Dream*

Amy J. Riess and George W. Williams

One of the central themes of *Romeo and Juliet*, of course, is that of young love between members of feuding families. The immediate source of Shakespeare's play, Brooke's *The Tragical History of Romeus and Juliet*, was only one of many works of the Renaissance and Elizabethan era that dealt with this theme, which harkened back to the stories of Pyramis and Thisbe (or Thisby) and Hero and Leander in Greek mythology. The Roman poet Ovid penned his own versions of these stories and his works became widely popular later; Shakespeare was most familiar with Elizabethan writer Arthur Golding's translation of Ovid. In the following essay, Shakespearean scholars Amy Riess and George Williams indirectly examine Shakespeare's creative use of the Pyramus and Thisbe theme, by offering a convincing argument that the presentation of the playlet "Pyramus and Thisby" by the bumpkin actors in *A Midsummer Night's Dream* was intended as a spoof of his own tragic telling of the same tale in *Romeo and Juliet*.

Perhaps Queen Mab gallops through critics' brains, and then they dream of the chronology of Shakespeare's plays—especially the sequence of *Romeo and Juliet* and *A Midsummer Night's Dream*. Editors of either of these two plays are inclined to consider the play that they are editing the later play. . . . Critics have argued for dating on the basis of natural events, such as earthquake, flood, and marriage, or of rhetorical elements, such as rhyme and vocabulary, but their efforts seem not yet to have settled the argument to everyone's satisfaction. This paper will argue from internal

From "'Tragical Mirth': From *Romeo* to *Dream*" by Amy J. Riess and George W. Williams, *Shakespeare Quarterly*, vol. 43, no. 2, Summer 1992. Reprinted by permission of the authors and the *Shakespeare Quarterly*.

evidence that *Romeo and Juliet* is the earlier play, and that in writing *A Midsummer Night's Dream*, Shakespeare used the events and the language of tragedy to increase the mirth of comedy. Whether or not he did so deliberately is beyond our knowledge, but some relationships are inescapably demonstrable. Most of these must have been unconscious in Shakespeare's mind; a few—as we see the matter—would seem to derive significance from a conscious awareness of the effect that the familiar knowledge of the earlier play would have on an audience in its response to the later play, such a knowledge perhaps shaping, certainly enriching, that response.

THE WALL IN "PYRAMUS AND THISBY"

Though many of the relationships between *Romeo and Juliet* and *A Midsummer Night's Dream* have been noted, some merit further consideration, particularly those concerning the playlet "Pyramus and Thisby," a text derived from Golding's version of Ovid's *Metamorphoses*, Book 4, lines 55–166. The first of these is the relationship between the parents of the young lovers, represented in the performance before the court in Athens by the erecting of a wall, symbolizing the parents' hostility, and by the later removal of that wall, symbolizing their reconciliation—a reconciliation effected by the deaths of their children. . . .

In the original casting of the playlet, in Act 1, scene 2, of *A Midsummer Night's Dream*, Peter Quince announces that he will take the part of Thisby's father, and he assigns the part of Pyramus' father to Tom Snout, the tinker. In Act 3, scene 1, the two mechanicals assigned the parts of the fathers, the counterparts of Capulet and Montague, are the first to refer to the wall. Quince (Thisby's father) recognizes that there must be "a wall in the great chamber; for Pyramus and Thisby, says the story, did talk through the chink of a wall," and Snout (Pyramus' father) retorts, "You can never bring in a wall." But in the performance, those parents do not appear; and hence there can be no hostility between them. Nevertheless, Shakespeare retains the wall to divide Pyramus and Thisby as a symbol of the divisive feud between the Montagues and Capulets. Juliet specifically has layered the walls with a mortar of mortality and has linked them with the deaths that result from the feud of the families:

> The orchard walls are high and hard to climb,
> And the place death, considering who thou art,

If any of my kinsmen find thee here.

The language and context of passages concerning the wall in the playlet betray the fact that Shakespeare had these fatal "orchard walls" of *Romeo and Juliet* in mind when he fashioned the "witty partition" of "Pyramus and Thisby."

And though there is no need to bring in a wall, in Act 5 Snout himself plays the part of Wall. In giving the part of Wall to Snout, a tinker, Shakespeare may have been taking into account the customary deprecatory attitude toward tinkers as unskilled menders. In such unskillfulness Snout as Wall may represent the continuing hostility (not easily mended) between the feuding families imported from *Romeo and Juliet.* In the wandering Wall of "Pyramus and Thisby," Shakespeare perpetuates the feud of *Romeo and Juliet.* Wall concludes his speaking part: "Thus have I, Wall, my part discharged so; / And, being done, thus Wall away doth go." Wall exits, and Theseus indicates symbolically the end of the feud:

ASSIGNING THE PARTS FOR "PYRAMUS AND THISBY"

In this portion of act 1, scene 2 of Shakespeare's A Midsummer Night's Dream, *Quince the carpenter hands out the parts for the upcoming amateur performance of "Pyramus and Thisby."*

Enter QUINCE *the carpenter and* SNUG *the joiner and* BOTTOM *the weaver and* FLUTE *the bellows-mender and* SNOUT *the tinker and* STARVELING *the tailor.*

QUIN. Is all our company here?

BOT. You were best to call them generally, man by man, according to the scrip.

QUIN. Here is the scroll of every man's name which is thought fit, through all Athens, to play in our enterlude before the Duke and the Duchess, on his wedding-day at night.

BOT. First, good Peter Quince, say what the play treats on; then read the names of the actors; and so grow to a point.

QUIN. Marry, our play is *The most lamentable comedy and most cruel death of Pyramus and Thisby.*

BOT. A very good piece of work, I assure you, and a merry. Now, good Peter Quince, call forth your actors by the scroll. Masters, spread yourselves.

QUIN. Answer as I call you. Nick Bottom the weaver.

BOT. Ready. Name what part I am for, and proceed.

QUIN. You, Nick Bottom, are set down for Pyramus.

BOT. What is Pyramus? a lover, or a tyrant?

"Now is the mural down between the two neighbors." But Wall reenters at the end of the playlet, retaining his association with the fatal feud, for Demetrius observes that Wall, along with Moonshine and Lion, will "bury the dead." This observation provokes Lion's assurance, for a second time, that "the wall is down that parted their fathers," and that the feud has come to an end. The barrier between feuding parents—not in Ovid, not in *A Midsummer Night's Dream*, not in "Pyramus and Thisby"—must allude to a situation that the audience would have recognized: the "Pyramus and Thisby" playlet deconstructs the wall of *Romeo and Juliet* hostility and ends with *Romeo and Juliet* reconciliation.

LINKS OF PROLOGUE AND DICTION

Another link between the tragedy and the playlet which may indicate precedence is the alteration of Quince's prologue so that in details it agrees with the prologue of *Romeo and*

QUIN. A lover, that kills himself most gallant for love.

BOT. That will ask some tears in the true performing of it. If I do it, let the audience look to their eyes. I will move storms; I will condole in some measure. . . .

QUIN. Francis Flute the bellows-mender.

FLU. Here, Peter Quince.

QUIN. Flute, you must take Thisby on you.

FLU. What is Thisby? a wand'ring knight?

QUIN. It is the lady that Pyramus must love.

FLU. Nay, faith; let not me play a woman; I have a beard coming.

QUIN. That's all one; you shall play it in a mask, and you may speak as small as you will.

BOT. And I may hide my face, let me play Thisby too. I'll speak in a monstrous little voice. "Thisne! Thisne! Ah, Pyramus, my lover dear! thy Thisby dear, and lady dear!"

QUIN. No, no, you must play Pyramus; and, Flute, you Thisby.

BOT. Well, proceed.

QUIN. Robin Starveling the tailor.

STAR. Here, Peter Quince.

QUIN. Robin Starveling, you must play Thisby's mother. Tom Snout the tinker.

SNOUT. Here, Peter Quince.

QUIN. You, Pyramus' father; myself, Thisby's father.

Juliet. In Act 3, scene 1, Quince announces, "Well, we will have . . . a prologue, and it shall be written in eight and six," and Bottom offers the alternative meter of eight and eight; but neither form is used for the prologue of the actual "Pyramus and Thisby" performance in Act 5. Quince writes in ten and ten (iambic pentameter) and so conforms the "Pyramus and Thisby" prologue to the metrics of the *Romeo and Juliet* prologue. Quince's prologue begins and ends with units of ten lines, each consisting of two quatrains and a final couplet. . . . But between these two "stanzaic" forms occurs a section of fourteen lines (plus one), replicating the rhyme scheme of the Elizabethan sonnet that constitutes the prologue of *Romeo and Juliet,* with, however, an extra line (unrhymed) interpolated before the final couplet, thereby "improving" on the standard sonnet form: "This grisly beast (which Lion hight by name)." Perhaps Quince adds this extra lion-line to accommodate Snout, who declared at the rehearsal, "Therefore another prologue must tell he is not a lion." Snug, as the Lion, delivers his own prologue later. . . .

A third link between *Romeo and Juliet* and "Pyramus and Thisby" occurs in the diction common to both plays. Although not all of these language parallels advance the precedence of either play, some clearly do, demonstrating the priority of *Romeo and Juliet.* The "hempen homespuns" speak the broken yet recognizable language of *Romeo and Juliet* in their farcical rendition of Shakespeare's earlier play, garbling the phrases from the tragedy to achieve grand comedy. In *Romeo and Juliet* the lovers utter the word "come" when haplessly they attempt to circumvent their fates. Romeo says "Come, cordial and not poison" after he defies the stars and the consequence there hanging and departs for Juliet's tomb, and Juliet says "Romeo, I come!" before she drinks her sleeping potion. In the playlet, Pyramus and Thisby embellish the language of *Romeo and Juliet* by twice repeating their calls to "come." At the sight of Thisby's mantle, Pyramus cries, "Approach, ye Furies fell! / O Fates, come, come," and Thisby, in concomitant mawkishness, addresses the Fates: "O Sisters Three, / Come, come to me."

The muddled language of "Pyramus and Thisby" evokes the death scenes of *Romeo and Juliet.* Romeo's "Thus with a kiss I die" provides a suitable example for Pyramus. Pyramus takes Romeo's simple but dramatic and suggestive "thus" and "die" and with great panache begins and ends his farewell, "Thus die I, thus, thus, thus.... Now die, die, die, die, die."

SHAKESPEARE MOCKS HIMSELF?

In what is perhaps an even more telling manifestation of dependence, the seeming deaths of Juliet and Thisby beg comparison. In the tragedy, Capulet mourns what he believes to be the death of Juliet, using the personification of Death as lover, and laments to Paris that Death has lain with Juliet: "Flower as she was, deflowered by him." In ludicrous fashion Pyramus mourns what he believes to be the death of Thisby, using—as it were—the same image: "Since lion vile hath here deflow'red my dear . . .". The image of Death as lover, borrowed from *Romeo and Juliet* and here associated in "Pyramus and Thisby" with a lion, is absurd: a lion may quail, crush, conclude, or quell a maiden but not, one supposes, deflower her. This "reinterpretation" is the more striking because the word "deflower" is itself a revamping of Golding's word "Devour." That Shakespeare changed "devour" to "deflower" so that Pyramus could echo Capulet seems certain. The word "deflower" occurs nowhere else in the canon [the compilation of Shakespeare's works] except in *Titus Andronicus* and *Measure for Measure.* That rarity unites *Romeo* and *Dream* inextricably, and the inappropriateness of the usage in *A Midsummer Night's Dream* argues strongly that the appropriate usage preceded in *Romeo and Juliet.* . . .

That it was fitting for Shakespeare to mock his earlier tragedy in his "Pyramus and Thisby" playlet is reasonable; Shakespeare parodies his own work in just such a fashion in *1 Henry IV*, where the serious scene of domestic banter between Hotspur and Lady Percy in 2.3 is derided through Prince Hal's mockery in 2.4. It would be difficult to argue that these treatments of the same event could be reversed.

In fact, the lovers from Ovid do not participate in Shakespeare's earlier play. Thisby is mentioned in *Romeo and Juliet*, but her actual presence there would be as unsuitable as is the taunting of Mercutio. Ignorant of Romeo's love for Juliet and teasing his friend about his unrequited love for Rosaline—the wrong lady—Mercutio refers to Thisby as having "a grey eye or so, but not to the purpose." After that rejection, Shakespeare writes a playlet "to the purpose," a story of more woe, for Thisby and her Pyramus (with eyes as "green as leeks") in *A Midsummer Night's Dream.*

The Meaning of the Night Visit in the Balcony Scenes

Jill Colaco

The "Night Visit," in which a man visits a woman, usually beneath her bedroom window, during formal courtship ritual, has been a part of European folklore for thousands of years. The scene has several specific, standard elements, including references to birds singing, torches or lamps burning, the dawn breaking, and folk songs about the breaking dawn (aubades). In this essay, Harvard University scholar Jill Colaco explains Shakespeare's use of the Night Visit in the famous balcony scenes (which she calls the Plighting Scene and the Parting Scene) of *Romeo and Juliet*, making the point that, even seeing the play for the first time, his Elizabethan audiences found both the scenes and their separate elements readily recognizable; by contrast, she suggests, modern audiences do not usually realize that Shakespeare's setting of these scenes drew upon ancient romantic traditions.

The love story of Romeo and Juliet is rooted in European folklore, though Shakespeare took his version directly from the unpromising pages of a long and elaborate verse-romance, which he transformed so compellingly that his lovers became the new legend. Critics attempting to account for the spellbinding power of the play frequently turn to the Window Scenes (II.ii and III.v) to speculate on the nature of the bond between the lovers. This paper is also concerned with those twin centers of the play, and with the important and undervalued Night Visit element that threads its way through the two intimate dialogues of plighting and parting. For *Romeo* and *Juliet*, with all its sophistication, draws on a

From "The Window Scenes in *Romeo and Juliet* and Folk Songs of the Night Visit" by Jill Colaco, *Studies in Philology*, vol. 83, no. 2, Spring 1986. Copyright ©1986 by the University of North Carolina Press. Used by permission of the publisher.

popular tradition in keeping with the story's folklore origins.

The conventions of the Night Visit would have been familiar to Elizabethans from drama and folksong, so the primary purpose of the following pages is to restore to a modern audience the ability to recognize and respond to the motif. My argument has a further place in the context of recent writing on *Romeo and Juliet,* which has greatly concerned itself with the nature of the love affair, and stressed the legitimacy and spirituality of the union. A new appreciation of the Night Visit motif is a reminder that Romeo and Juliet, even after their wedding, are conducting a clandestine liaison that has more in common with a dangerous intrigue than with a licit marriage.

I would not want to deny the significance of the sacred and nuptial language in the love scenes; my contention is rather that the play embraces many different kinds of lovemaking, and that Romeo and Juliet's feelings are expressed through a greater range of modes than any single critic will admit. H.A. Mason [author of *Shakespeare's Tragedies of Love*], for instance, interprets the balcony scene as a "scene of plighting rather than love"; in this paper, having decided to rename the scene in order to avoid the scholarly dispute about the balcony, I have called it the Plighting Scene as a tribute to Mason's insight. But this is a large oversimplification of a long meeting, in which perpetual modulations in the lovers' language play endlessly against the visual language of the striking set.

Placing Romeo beneath his sweetheart's window in the moonlight puts him in the role of a serenader in the first stages of courtship; his soliloquy does indeed come from the serenader's impulse to sing in praise of his lady's beauty, even though on this occasion he does not expect to be heard. Romeo is also a lover in the *Song of Songs* [or Song of Solomon, one of the books of the Old Testament, containing verses of love] and Courtly Love tradition, with Juliet at her window as the beloved in the walled garden and the lady in the castle tower. In the Parting Scene, it is no surprise to learn that in this walled orchard there are a nightingale and a pomegranate tree, since both are common accessories of the *Song of Songs* tradition. But an Elizabethan audience would have picked up yet other cues from the staging, associating it immediately with the well-known and less elevated scenario of the Night Visit.

The image of Romeo as the importunate lover of Night Visit folksong need not cancel out the rest: the *Song of Songs* is as strongly associated with the Night Visit as with Courtly Love, and the overlapping of the uncertain serenader with the bolder lover is a way of telescoping all the phases appropriate to a more extended wooing. It does, however, subvert the nuptial interpretation of the play that seeks to rarefy the love affair and heightens the sanctioned marriage at the expense of the secret romance.

POISED BETWEEN COMEDY AND TRAGEDY

The paradigm of the Night Visit . . . goes something like this. The man makes the woman aware of his presence outside and asks her to let him in. The woman responds at first with surprise or disapproval. . . . But after the standard prevarication, the song usually ends with the woman relenting and inviting her lover to enter. . . .

The song is constructed around the man's repeated "Open the door" pleas or the woman's "Go from my window" refrain. In either case, the man's desperation or the woman's intransigence is suddenly reversed by the woman admitting her sweetheart to the house. The exchange is a kind of ritual, and the outcome is rarely in doubt. The comic potential of this predictable change of heart has been repeatedly exploited by storytellers and dramatists. Chaucer's *Miller's Tale* [from his larger *Canterbury Tales*] is a memorable instance of a double reversal, for Alisoun initially refuses to play the yielding part of a "Go from my window" singer . . . and then pretends to relent in order to set up the ardent Absolon for an even bigger surprise. But most of the folk songs are not comic; indeed, in many of the longer Child Ballads, the threat to the lovers is real, and their meeting may have fatal consequences.

The opening of a Night Visit sequence can clearly be heard in the first words addressed by Juliet to the man under her window. Unlike the heroines in Shakespeare's sources, who immediately recognize their sweethearts in the moonlight, this Juliet responds to Romeo's sudden declaration with the challenge:

> What man art thou that thus bescreen'd in night
> So stumblest on my counsel?

The dialogue that follows has affinities with both the lighter folk songs and the darker ballads of the Night Visit, befitting a scene that is precariously poised between comedy and tragedy. The thrill of danger found in the Child Ballads is lurking here in the Capulets' garden, and Juliet repeatedly expresses her fears:

> And the place death, considering who thou art,
> If any of my kinsmen find thee here . . .
> If they do see thee, they will murder thee . . .
> I would not for the world they saw thee here.

. . . Towards the end of the Plighting Scene, the comic possibilities of the situation resurface. The interruption of the lovers' exchange by the Nurse—which is again without parallel in Shakespeare's sources—is reminiscent of the shorter Night Visit songs, where the risk of interference by the mother or father is comically treated:

> JULIET.
> I hear some noise within. Dear love, adieu.
> [*Nurse calls within.*]
> Anon, good Nurse—Sweet Montague be true.
> Stay but a little, I will come again . . .
> NURSE. [*Within.*] Madam.
> JULIET. I come, anon—But if thou meanest not well
> I do beseech thee—
> NURSE. [*Within.*] Madam.
> JULIET.   By and by I come—

. . . In the play, as in the comparable folk songs, it is obvious that no hurt is going to come to the lovers through the Nurse's unwanted proximity; they are in the protected garden of comedy into which an authority figure cannot harmfully intrude. This is a different world from the Child Ballads where murderous kinsmen threaten the lovers' lives, yet the two traditions are related and Shakespeare's scene encompasses them both. . . .

As the Plighting Scene draws to a close, Juliet's repeated recalling of Romeo traces the old Night Visit pattern of the woman's last-minute recalling of the suitor she had dismissed. And as the lovers reluctantly part and Romeo makes his speech to "The grey-ey'd morn," night merges into day and Night Visit gives way to aubade [a song about daybreak].

BORROWING FROM OTHERS

There is convincing evidence that these Night Visit motifs were readily available to Elizabethan dramatists in popular English folksong. In an important article, which I have used extensively in this study, Charles Read Baskervill admits that extant Night Visit songs are tantalizingly rare in Britain, but his wide-ranging research nevertheless builds up a case for the existence of a strong native tradition going back to the Middle Ages: "These conventions of the night visit, though simple and natural enough in themselves, recur so persistently in different types of popular poetry as to suggest that to the popular mind the theme called for the use of certain formulas, and that back of the few examples . . . recorded early there lay a considerable body of song which had arisen among the folk.". . .

Albert B. Friedman is one of the recent scholars to stress the [Elizabethan] dramatists' extensive use of folksong material: "The numerous quotations and allusions made by Elizabethan and Jacobean playwrights to popular songs show that they expected their audiences to be intimately familiar with a great mass of such stuff." Shakespeare's own irrepressible interest in folksong manifests itself in many of his plays; *Hamlet* includes a fascinating example of a bawdy branch of the Night Visit tradition in Ophelia's "To-morrow is Saint Valentine's day," an "Open the door" song about the one night in the year when the woman had the customary right to be the wooer. . . .

Other Elizabethan playwrights before Shakespeare had also explored the dramatic possibilities of the Night Visit. In [sixteenth-century English poet Anthony] Munday's *Fidele and Fortunio: The Two Italian Gentlemen* (1584), the heroine Victoria makes several appearances at her window, and the plot turns on multiple actual or suspected Night Visits. *Fidele and Fortunio* may in fact have been one of the plots that Shakespeare had in mind when he wrote *Much Ado [About Nothing]*, where the accusations against Hero depend upon a faked Night Visit. He had definitely been impressed by the nocturnal encounter in [sixteenth-century English writer Christopher] Marlowe's *The Jew of Malta*, which he used in *The Merchant of Venice* in the scene in which Shylock's daughter awaits her lover at a window. Editors of *Romeo and Juliet* have long been aware of possible borrowings from Marlowe in the Plighting Scene, but little attention has been given to the shaping of both dialogues around the scenario of the Night Visit.

In Marlowe's play, Barabas the Jew is prowling around a nunnery, yearning for a glimpse not of a sweetheart but of his daughter Abigail, who has become a novice to recover the wealth hidden in the house. Abigail enters "above," and after four alternating speeches during which she and her father (like Romeo and Juliet at the opening of the Plighting Scene) remain oblivious of each other's presence, Barabas catches sight of her. . . . Like Romeo, Barabas marks the end of the Night Visit with a fond flourish, and turns to greet the nearing day. . . . Shakespeare's imagination seems to have absorbed this dark, sardonic Night Visit and converted it into the lovely and innocent Plighting Scene. . . .

Romeo and Juliet, then, was written in what practically amounted to a theatre tradition of the Night Visit, and the examples I have described make it clear that the dramatic versions never left the folksong conventions far behind. . . .

NIGHT GIVES WAY TO DAWN

Even though the outline of the Plighting Scene follows the shape of a Night Visit song, beginning with the woman's challenge and ending with the recalling of her lover, it does not lead immediately to Romeo being admitted. When Juliet asks with wilful innocence, "What satisfaction canst thou have tonight?," the audience realizes—if the point has not already been made by the height of her window—that no hasty meeting will take place in her room on this occasion. There is, however, a strong feeling that the pattern will be completed, wedding or no wedding, and that Romeo's entry has merely been postponed. The Night Visit in *Romeo and Juliet* is split over two nights, and the incompleteness of the visit is one source of the suspense between the Plighting and Parting Scenes. Even when Romeo's banishment has been pronounced, the expectation that the lovers will yet have one night together is thereby kept alive.

The meeting takes place literally over the heads of Juliet's father and suitor, a constant reminder that the wedding ceremony has not wholly legitimized the lovers' relationship. Their married life begins without the sanction of family or society, and is more like the private betrothal meeting in which Night Visit songs probably originated than like the consummation of a legal and church-blessed union. . . .

The natural sequel to a stolen Night Visit is a Dawn Parting before the awakening of the family or the town. The European folk tradition is rich in love-lyrics which celebrate and lament the sweet sorrow of parting, and . . . the [plighting] scene has all the thematic and formal properties that place it in the mainstream of the aubade folk tradition. It can be paralleled in numerous places in European song, not only in its use of minor conventions—birdsong, hints of light, ingenious arguments denying the nearness of day, interruption by a friendly watcher—but also in its dynamics, the tension between the lovers' reluctance to accept the passing of night and their inevitable need to part.

Romeo and Juliet's debate about the lark and the nightingale has one interesting English analogy in the old Child Ballad, "Little Musgrave and Lady Barnard.". . .

> "Methinks I hear the thresel-cock,
> Methinks I hear the jaye;
> Methinks I hear my lord Barnard,
> And I would I were away."

> "Lye still, lye still, thou Little Musgrave,
> And huggell me from the cold;
> 'T is nothing but a shepherd's boy,
> A driving his sheep to the fold."

These stanzas capture the spirit of the aubade, the contradictory fears and desires of the couple, which border on comedy even as tragedy approaches: Little Musgrave is persuaded to stay and is killed by the returning husband. The Parting Scene is similarly set on a knife edge between make-believe and murder, and its brief reference to a hunt's-up is a further reminder of danger. Juliet urges Romeo to escape as if he were the huntsman's prey, with the words "Hie hence, begone, away," and later in the same speech says of the larksong:

> that voice doth us affray,
> Hunting thee hence with hunt's-up to the day. . . .

Shakespeare is evidently fishing in the same deep pool of images as the ballad-makers and, I suggest, not simply sharing universal poetic tropes, but actually inviting his audience to associate his lovers' words with the language and ways of folksong. . . .

Between the Plighting and Parting Scenes, the mood has changed, and reminders of the earlier Night Visit serve to underline the difference between that sweet parting and this bitter division. With the line, "The day is broke, be wary, look about" (III.v.40), the Nurse bursts in on the scene and rudely precipitates Romeo's departure; unable to continue the comic off-stage part of the Night Visit scenario, she is now needed to take on the more serious aubade role of the faithful watcher. When Romeo has reached the ground, the lovers are positioned as they were in the Plighting Scene; the Night Visit is now clearly over, and this heightens the finality of the lovers' farewells. Instead of anticipating Romeo's ascent, Juliet is now gazing down at the prospect of further descent and endless separation:

> O God, I have an ill-divining soul!
> Methinks I see thee, now thou art so low,
> As one dead in the bottom of a tomb.

It is fated that there will be a third Night Visit—the bizarre tryst in the tomb—when everything that folksong lovers fear becomes reality. The friendly watcher, Balthazar, fails to interrupt in time, the families and the town are aroused, and morning slowly breaks. But the unpartable lovers still lie together, indifferent to discovery by their kinsmen or the day.

Physical and Spiritual Sickness Infects the Lovers' World

David M. Bergeron

Though *Romeo and Juliet* contains literally hundreds of references to disease, illnesses of both body and spirit, and potential remedies for these maladies, few critics and scholars have examined this overriding theme of sickness in a unified way. David Bergeron, an English professor at the University of Kansas and editor of *Research Opportunities in Renaissance Drama*, does so here, pointing out that Shakespeare's thematic development of sickness in the play is perfectly consistent with, and indeed defines, the tragedy of the piece. "Tragedy is a function of illness and health," says Bergeron, maintaining that in comedy illness ultimately finds a cure, whereas in tragedy it does not. He describes medieval Verona, the lovers' world, as "infected and in need of healing." The tragedy, of course, is that the healing comes too late to help Romeo and Juliet.

If we have cut our critical teeth on tragedies like *The Spanish Tragedy* [1584, by Thomas Kyd], *Hamlet,* and *The Revenger's Tragedy* [1607, by Cyril Tourneur], we may have some difficulty in locating the tragic sense in *Romeo and Juliet.* Indeed some theatre directors choose to present it as a comedy, emphasizing Mercutio, the Nurse, and the sacrificial nature of the deaths of Romeo and Juliet which ultimately bring reconciliation of the Capulets and Montagues.... That this play differs markedly in design from *Hamlet, Othello, Lear,* and *Macbeth* is undeniable, but I believe that no degree of emphasis on sacrifice can truly mitigate the tragedy that occurs. The play in fact *becomes* a tragedy as it turns away from its comic possibilities. It finally

From "Sickness in *Romeo and Juliet*" by David M. Bergeron, *CLA Journal,* vol. 20, no. 3, March 1977. Reprinted by permission of the College Language Association.

more nearly resembles the Pyramus and Thisbe story than it does *A Midsummer Night's Dream.*

One of the imagery and thematic threads that run throughout Shakespeare's drama is sickness; in the tragedies illness is not susceptible to cure, while typically in the comedies a healing agent or device makes all whole. The concrete, physical examples of sickness are subsumed in the larger, metaphorical pattern which allows the dramatist to construct the play-world either with spiritual disease and corruption (tragedy) or with graceful healing and reconciliation (comedy). The remedies offered in tragedy are ineffective, while in comedy they are efficacious.

Despite the initial festive quality of *Romeo and Juliet*—its feasts, dances, love stories—the play abounds with images of sickness, boding the tragedy to come. This pattern of imagery has largely gone unnoticed [by literary critics], but I believe that it provides another means of defining the tragedy. Romeo gives a clue to the imagery in his first appearance. Outlining his troubled response to love for Rosaline, he sums up the nature of love in a series of oxymorons, including "Feather of lead, bright smoke, cold fire, sick health. . . ." While this may seem fairly tame and conventional stuff, the paradox of "sick health" is arresting, implying the threat to health which exists in this play as the images of disease and illness give rise to a tragic world of disorder, fragmentation, and finally death. The polarities of sickness and health suggest a tragic axis on which the play turns, and on the plot graph of this play tragedy is a function of illness and health. In the analysis which follows, one can chart both the categories of disease and the attempts at remedies, thereby answering in one way at least, how the play is tragic.

A FESTERING SORE BETWEEN THE HOUSEHOLDS

The maladies in the play may be categorized as illness of body, of spirit, and of body politic. The physical ailments cover a rather wide range of problems with varying degrees of seriousness: the bump on the head which Juliet received as a child; the corns mentioned by the elder Capulet at the dance; the suggestion by Mercutio that Romeo may have the pox; the aching bones, backache, and headache suffered by the Nurse; Juliet's anemia; the unruly spleen mentioned by Benvolio; Tybalt's onslaught of choler; Romeo's vague "distemp'rature." In addition to actual problems the characters are aware of the crucial importance of health. As the Capulet household busies itself with preparation for Juliet's forthcoming wedding to Paris, the Nurse urges Capulet to get to bed: "Faith, you'll be sick to-morrow / For this night's watching." But he insists on his health: "What, I have watched ere now / All night for lesser cause, and ne'er been sick." That boast turns back upon him with sharp irony as a few minutes later he learns of the apparent death of Juliet. When Balthasar arrives at Mantua in V.i, Romeo's first questions and statements concern health: "Is my father well? / How fares my Juliet? That I ask again / For nothing can be ill if she be well." But of course Balthasar brings "ill news."

Individually considered, the physical maladies may not seem very important, but collectively they add to the tragic tone and epitomize a world infected and in need of healing. There are at least two instances of physical sickness which are dramatically crucial and which help determine the tragedy. One is the shedding of blood in III.i, the moment at which the play clearly turns toward a tragic inevitability. Benvolio notes in the opening lines that there is "mad blood stirring" in Verona, and within a few minutes that mad blood manifests itself in the deaths of Mercutio and Tybalt, reminding one of the words in the Prologue that civil blood would make civil hands unclean. Mercutio's cry for a surgeon goes unheeded; and his curse of "A plague o' both your houses!" may have more literal tinge to it than one usually thinks. In the next scene, III.ii, the Nurse reports to Juliet the horrible events that have happened, emphasizing the wounds and blood she has observed. Coming as it does shortly after the marriage of Romeo and Juliet in II.vi, this new sickness is juxtaposed paradoxically to the potential health implicit in the lovers' wedding, thus echoing Romeo's early oxymoron of "sick health." Medically, the shedding of blood is often necessary and may lead to healing, but ironically in the play this event is both cause and effect of sickness—the ultimate result of a festering sore between the households and the trigger to further tragic action.

The series of physical illnesses culminates dramatically in the report of Friar John in V.ii, that he did not get to Mantua because in the name of visiting the sick in Verona he and a fellow friar were sealed up in a house suspected of containing "the infectious pestilence." An actual sickness has thus prevented the dramatically crucial letter from reaching Romeo. Shakespeare's device here seems perfectly consistent with the pervasive images and reports of illness. Thus in III.i, with the shedding of blood and here in V.ii, with the plague, all possibilities for averting tragedy are lost, and we now await the inevitable. While on a worthy mission Friar John is detained in a house of apparent pestilence, as Romeo

THE FRIAR GATHERS MEDICINAL HERBS

In this speech, featured in the opening of act 2, scene 3, Friar Laurence, who is out in the fields gathering herbs, equates poison with medicine, showing us that, though he is well meaning and fancies himself a healer, he is doomed to kill rather than cure his patients.

FRIAR. The grey-eyed morn smiles on the frowning night,
Chequ'ring the Eastern clouds with streaks of light;
And flecked darkness like a drunkard reels
From forth day's path and Titan's fiery wheels.
Now, ere the sun advance his burning eye
The day to cheer and night's dank dew to dry,
I must up-fill this osier cage of ours
With baleful weeds and precious-juiced flowers.
The earth that's nature's mother is her tomb,
What is her burying grave, that is her womb;
And from her womb children of divers kind
We sucking on her natural bosom find;
Many for many virtues excellent,
None but for some, and yet all different.
O, mickle is the powerful grace that lies
In plants, herbs, stones, and their true qualities;
For naught so vile that on the earth doth live
But to the earth some special good doth give;
Nor aught so good but, strained from that fair use,
Revolts from true birth, stumbling on abuse.
Virtue itself turns vice, being misapplied,
And vice sometime's by action dignified.
Within the infant rind of this small flower
Poison hath residence, and medicine power;
For this, being smelt, with that part cheers each part;
Being tasted, slays all senses with the heart.
Two such opposed kings encamp them still
In man as well as herbs—grace and rude will;
And where the worser is predominant,
Full soon the canker death eats up that plant.

and Juliet with their own worthy motives will be sealed in the tomb of death.

SICKNESS OF SPIRIT

Though emotional stress of various degrees afflicts a number of characters, the sickness of spirit most discussed is lovesickness, which has both its literal and figurative aspects. It is, of course, an illness frequent in Shakespearean comedy, for example, in Duke Orsino in *Twelfth Night.* Before Romeo enters the play, his kinsmen discuss his condition, the humor that troubles him. Montague tells Benvolio: "Could we but learn from whence his sorrows grow, / We would as willingly give cure as know." It is soon clear that Romeo suffers from love, which he characterizes as "a madness most discreet." Benvolio urges him to discuss the problem, but Romeo responds: "Bid a sick man in sadness make his will. / Ah, word ill urged to one that is so ill!" Later Romeo points out that he has been wounded by love, "enpierced with his shaft. . . ." The more profound ailment comes of course in his new love for Juliet, having survived the "sickness" for Rosaline. Romeo opens the famous balcony scene with reference to sickness: "He jests at scars that never felt a wound." When he sees Juliet, he likens her to the sun that kills the envious moon, "Who is already sick and pale with grief"—this moon whose "vestal livery is but sick and green." But Juliet's premonitions here and in III.v imply the threat to their healthy love; her "ill-divining soul" is alert to the troublesome paradox of sick health.

From the Prologue which opens the play to the closing lines of the drama, a metaphorical sickness in the body politic envelops the world of Verona, namely, the ancient grudge between the Capulets and Montagues, which finally spawns heartbreaks and death. The fact of these warring houses frames the action, implying the disorderly and unhealthy world of Verona. Only the deaths of Romeo and Juliet finally expunge the illness, but, of course, at a great and tragic price. Though in some sense the play is a "domestic tragedy," the larger, external world of the festering conflict between families is forever colliding with the will of the lovers. The public conflict in I.i, and III.i, finds its counterpart in the private resentment expressed in the Capulet festive scene in I.v, where the rash Tybalt recognizes Romeo as a Montague, "our foe" and would "strike him dead" for the family's honor. At the play's end the Prince points out to the Capulets and Montagues: "See what a scourge is laid upon your hate, / That heaven finds means to kill your joys with love." The tomb offers mute testimony to the destructive illness that has infected the households.

POTENTIAL REMEDIES

But what about the attempts at healing? Remedies, prescriptions, and "physicians" are present, but singly or collectively they fail. The breathless and aching Nurse in II.v, asks for a "poultice" but receives none. Feeling her woes and sorrows, she asks for "aqua vitae," but to no avail. And when the Nurse discovers the seemingly dead Juliet, she again cries out for "Some aqua vitae"; but such a prescription is pointless. The dying Mercutio asks for a surgeon, but none is to be found. Thus even these practical maladies and wounds know no healing.

Resorting to the Friar for help, Juliet receives his prescription, a potion which will induce a death-like state. This medicine suggests a way of gaining health for the distraught couple; but in the privacy of her chamber Juliet wonders: "What if it be a poison which the friar / Subtly hath minist'red to have me dead...." It is no poison, though its effect aggravates rather than cures the situation. Certainly Juliet's parents must assume that she is dead; and death, not Paris, is the ostensible bridegroom. Laying rosemary on the corpse takes the place of the expected festive wedding.

The prescription most often discussed and finally sought to resolve the ills of the play-world is poison, underscored by the fourteen times that the word is used in the play—the highest incidence in all of Shakespeare's drama.... In one of this play's most important thematic speeches Friar Laurence notes that within the flower that he holds, "Poison hath residence, and medicine power...." There is no clearer statement of the paradox of "sick health." As with the flower, so with the play: comedy and tragedy are potential in the same situation; healing could come, or poison work its fatal power. When night's candles have burned out and Romeo parts from Juliet at their last meeting, Juliet assumes the role of outrage at this man who has killed her kinsman Tybalt. She says to her mother: "... I never shall be satisfied / With Romeo till I behold him—dead..."; and she promises that if a man could be found "To bear a poison," she would "temper it" and offer it to Romeo. Surely these words must haunt Juliet in that final moment in the tomb as she awakens to find her Romeo indeed poisoned. . . .

As we know, poison in the closing scene of the play seals the tragic doom of the lovers. Preparing to drink the fatal potion, Romeo refers to it as "bitter conduct," "unsavory guide"; and he sees his "seasick weary bark" as now run aground on the dashing rocks. He drinks and exclaims with a fine ambiguity: "O true apothecary! / Thy drugs are quick. Thus with a kiss I die." Juliet finds the cup of poison and chides her lover for not having left a "friendly drop" for her; so she kisses the lips, hoping to find poison "To make me die with a restorative," echoing her lover who called the poison a "cordial." By this point in the action the lovers are willing to distort meaning, to designate that which kills them as a balm for their weary souls. But there is no health for them. The axis of "sick health" has become a polarity with tragic waste pre-empting comic fruitfulness and life. . . .

DEATH AND CONTAGION PREVAIL

At the dramatic and thematic center of the search for a cure is Friar Laurence, but he too is ultimately unsuccessful; in fact, he, ironically, exacerbates the illness. In his speech in II.iii, he observes the conflict between medicine and poison, the paradox of sick health. He finds in nature both "baleful weeds" and "precious-juiced flowers," a dazzling array of contraries. Noting the duality in nature, he can also perceive it in men, the tension between "grace and rude will"; "And where the worser is predominant, / Full soon the canker death eats up that plant"—health gives way to sickness. So perceptive a person has the capacity to reconcile, to heal; his failure to do so is another measure of the play as a tragedy.

When Romeo in the first flush of his new-found love for Juliet arrives at the Friar's cell, the Friar immediately senses that something is wrong, believing that Romeo is "uproused with some distemp'rature. . . ." But Romeo says that he and Juliet suffer only the wound of love, and he pinpoints the problems for the Friar: "Both our remedies / Within thy help and holy physic lies." This man who understands the medicinal power of herbs is now called on for spiritual medicine, and indeed he hopes to turn the family rancor into love. He understands the potential for a universal spiritual cure; thus he consents to perform the sacrament of marriage for

Romeo and Juliet, with all its healthy, "comic" possibilities.

But the frantic Romeo who confronts the Friar in III.iii, is suicidal: "Hadst thou no poison mixed, no sharp-ground knife, / No sudden mean of death. . . ." Friar Laurence calms Romeo's agitated spirit and sketches a strategy, a possible cure, that will permanently and safely unite the lovers. In her final speech of Act III Juliet sets out to the Friar's cell: "I'll to the friar to know his remedy." And she greets him in IV.i: "Come weep with me—past hope, past cure, past help!" She cries out for a "remedy," and the Friar says: ". . . if thou darest, I'll give thee remedy." He gives Juliet the potion and dispatches letters to Romeo in Mantua. Tragically, the cure does not work, and the holy physician must watch his patients die. His final suggestion of escape to Juliet in the tomb goes unheeded; instead death and contagion prevail. Friar Laurence is not the cause of the sickness in the play, but he is able to do little to assuage it. Given the sickness prevalent in the play, both physical and metaphorical, and the ineffective prescriptions and physicians, there can be little doubt of the tragic action and tragic spirit.

Social Restrictions Against Illicit Unions in *Romeo and Juliet*

Ann J. Cook

In late Renaissance England, the society in which Shakespeare lived and wrote, a number of social restrictions concerned illicit male-female relationships, most especially those involving sexual relations before marriage, but also adultery, secret marriages, elopements, and so forth. It is not surprising that this kind of social intolerance was a frequent theme of his works; and the theme is especially well developed in *Romeo and Juliet*, set in Renaissance Italy where such intolerance for deviations from the normal courting and marriage customs was very strong. In this essay, Ann J. Cook, a professor of English at Vanderbilt University and chairwoman of the International Shakespeare Association, explains how the social restrictions censoring illicit unions in his own and other European societies made Shakespeare very careful to show, from the outset, that Romeo's and Juliet's relationship is honorable and sanctified by marriage.

Though the conventional steps leading to an indissoluble marriage seemed clear enough to English subjects [in Shakespeare's time], there were also shortcuts, detours, and journeys abandoned altogether. In some cases, lovers made private rather than public promises to marry. And whatever the nature of their espousals, couples could and did consummate unions without waiting for a religious ceremony. Legally binding contracts . . . might be set aside if any of several impediments existed. Elopements and secret weddings sometimes occurred. Under certain circumstances marriages were annulled, and on a few grounds even a form of

divorce was possible. But because such situations represented a departure from prescribed behavior, a plethora of
opinion, advice, legal restrictions, social stigma, and economic punishments converged upon those who strayed from
the more conventional ways of making a match.

Of particular concern was the danger of clandestine meet-
ings between an unmarried man and woman lest they lead
to sexual intercourse. The Elizabethans' great fear of seduction derived from the ensuing stain on the female's reputation, the likelihood of pregnancy, and the possibility of her
subsequent abandonment. At every level, the social structure
required a child to be supported by his parents so he would
not become a charge on the general public. Hence, church
courts prosecuted with vigor cases of bastardy, fornication,
prenuptial pregnancy, and adultery. The homily *Against
Whoredom and Uncleanness* was read in every parish, there
were legal penalties for harboring unwed mothers, pregnancy meant dismissal for unwed servants, and midwives
were instructed to use extreme means during labor for determining the fathers of illegitimate children. . . . Not surpris-
ingly, the records show a low incidence of illegitimacy—
about 3 percent or less, though a small upsurge around the
turn of the century has not been fully explained. . . .

WARNINGS AGAINST IMPROPRIETY

For a woman, sexual seduction was the evil worse than
death. Among ordinary folk, chastity might or might not matter, but the importance of guaranteeing correct lines of in-
heritance and descent increased the significance of virginity
for wealthy and titled females. Stern are the warnings against
even the appearance of impropriety: "She ought also to be
more circumspect and to take better heed that she give no occasion to be yll reported of, and so to beehave her selfe, that
she be not onlye not spotted wyth anye fault, but not so much
as with suspicion." The maidenhead is regarded as "brittle
ware, which vnlesse your care be the greater for the preser-
uation, may get a cracke that no Art of man can make whole
againe, and a blow, that no herbe is of sufficient efficacy to
cure.". . . Those who lose their virginity are denounced as
"Monsters," "more vile then filthy channell durt fit to be
swept out of the heart and suburbes of your Countrey."

Because seduction could so easily masquerade as an intention to marry, secret betrothals came under particular

criticism and suspicion. As part of their regular duties, parish priests were to report "Whether you know any to have made privy contracts of Matrimony, not calling two or more witnesses thereunto, nor having thereto the consent of their Parents." These "privy contracts" were thought to derive from "knauery, falshood, and deceite ... wherby yong ignoraunt people are vtterly begiled and destroied.". . . . Not even a ring could unequivocally demonstrate a betrothal, especially if it were made of rush or some other perishable substance. Unless acknowledged by both parties or by witnesses, a private pledge had no legal standing, and it could be set aside if either partner were a minor. Still, some lovers did make clandestine commitments. . . .

HONORABLE INTENT FROM THE FIRST

[For these reasons] Shakespeare is especially careful about what he does and does not present in *Romeo and Juliet.* With two minors whose parents would violently oppose any alliance, it is essential to show how and why the young couple are truly married. Hence, the spectator sees, step by step, the

---

MARRIAGE IN RENAISSANCE ITALY

In this excerpt from his book Daily Life in Renaissance Italy, *scholar Charles L. Mee Jr. offers this overview of the social routine young people like Romeo and Juliet were expected to follow when getting married.*

The best a father could do with a female child was to have her married to advantage. An impoverished aristocratic family might use a daughter to gain a son of an up-and-coming merchant family; a nouveau-riche family might arrange to have a daughter marry into an old aristocratic family. . . . Women thus became one of the vehicles for social mobility—helping, by their arranged marriages, to balance and transfer economic and political power. All Renaissance Italians were busy matchmakers, and none were busier than the rulers of the city-states, who made and blocked marriages with a keen appreciation of the advantage or threat any marriage might hold to their power. . . .

No negotiation was more important than the negotiation of a marriage contract, and it might take months or years to conclude. A respectable dowry for a merchant's daughter amounted to about 1,000 florins in the fifteenth century, a

movement from the lovers' first encounter to their indissoluble union. In the balcony scene, Juliet repeatedly urges Romeo (and the audience) not to misjudge her morality: "In truth, fair Montague, I am too fond, / And therefore thou mayst think my 'havior light." "Therefore pardon me, / And not impute this yielding to light love." She assumes that with their mutual declarations of love, Romeo has made a private promise to marry her. Despite the physical impossibility of a handfasting, she even uses the correct legal term for their vows: "I have no joy of this *contract* tonight. / It is too rash, too unadvised, too sudden" (italics mine). By voicing the same misgivings that prudent adults might feel concerning her relationship with Romeo, Juliet establishes her purity as well as her passion. Though the only satisfaction Romeo asks that night is "Th'exchange of thy love's faithful vow for mine," she proposes that he prove his sincerity in the only ethical way possible:

> If that thy bent of love be honourable,
> Thy purpose marriage, send me word tomorrow,
> By one that I'll procure to come to thee,
> Where and what time thou wilt perform the rite,

good dowry, 1,500 florins—most of it in cash, some of it reckoned as the value of clothes and other possessions the bride brought with her. . . .

With a dowry of 1,000 florins, a young man could buy a quarter interest in a silk or wool shop, on which he would earn as much as 15 per cent, or 150 florins a year. If he combined his wife's dowry with funds put up by his brothers and cousins, he could get into the trade in foreign cloth . . . and become a distinguished citizen. . . .

Once the negotiations for marriage had been completed, a number of the relatives of the prospective bride and groom were assembled in church along with the intermediaries who had drawn up the marriage contract; the representatives of the two families confirmed the agreement by shaking hands—thus the name of the first ceremony of marriage, *impalmare*. . . . The bride did not appear at the *impalmare*; she appeared at the second ceremony, the betrothal, and then again at the third ceremony, which was held in her home. On this occasion a good many relatives and friends were invited to witness the exchange of vows and rings and to join in the wedding feast.

> And all my fortunes at thy foot I'll lay,
> And follow thee, my lord, throughout the world.

Yet she can still see the alternative interpretation of her wooer's behavior: "But if thou mean'st not well, / I do be-seech thee. . . . / To cease thy strife and leave me to my grief." In no other play do we get so clear a delineation of honor-able intent in an unsanctioned courtship, for the dynamics of *Romeo and Juliet* require a firm belief in the lovers' in-tegrity from first to last.

Further difficulties surround the wedding itself. First, a plausible explanation must be offered for any priest's willing-ness to officiate in such obviously irregular circumstances. Though chiding young Romeo for his impetuous commit-ment, Friar Laurence consents on reasonable grounds: "I'll thy assistant be; / For this alliance may so happy prove / To turn your households' rancour to pure love." A second prob-lem, common to most elopements, arises from the restricted movements of unmarried girls beyond their own households. Since Romeo has no direct access to Juliet . . . the Nurse be-comes the essential agent between the lovers. She utters the usual warning against seduction in the guise of courtship: "If ye should lead her in a fool's paradise, as they say, it were a very gross kind of behaviour, . . . truly it were an ill thing to be offered to any gentlewoman." However, what the hero has in mind is a lawful marriage. In sending the following message to Juliet via the Nurse, he clarifies the strategy that will effect an almost impossible union and its consummation.

> Bid her devise
> Some means to come to shrift this afternoon,
> And there she shall at Friar Laurence' cell
> Be shrived and married. . . .
> . . . .
> Within this hour my man shall be with thee
> And bring thee cords made like a tackled stair,
> Which to the high topgallant of my joy
> Must be my convoy in the secret night.

The excuse of going to confession is especially clever, for it offers Juliet a plausible reason to leave the Capulet house, it reasserts the lovers' virtue, and it satisfies the requirement for absolution before marriage. During the brief scene at Friar Laurence's cell, the same insistence upon the sanctity of the union appears, with Romeo's request to "close our hands with holy words" and the friar's directive, "Come, come with me, and we will make short work, / For, by your leaves, you shall not stay alone / Till Holy Church incorporate two in one."

SATISFYING CIVIL AND RELIGIOUS LAW

Here is no transitory dalliance or secret promise of love, rashly consummated, but rather a religious consecration of private vows between a virgin and her betrothed husband. Nor is it a questionable nighttime affair but rather one inaugurated in the broad light of day, though not before the canonical deadline of noon. While the union might still be annulled at this point, especially in view of Romeo's subsequent killing of Tybalt, Juliet reconfirms her commitment, vowing to "die maiden-widowed" if necessary and sending her bridegroom a ring as token of her fidelity. "O, find him! Give this ring to my true knight, / And bid him come to take his last farewell." That same night a sexual consummation makes Romeo and Juliet husband and wife forever. In a final touch of pathos, their fathers tender belated offers of dower and dowry over the bodies of two dead children.

> CAPULET. O brother Montague, give me thy hand.
> This is my daughter's jointure, for no more
> Can I demand.
>
> MONTAGUE.   But I can give thee more,
> For I will raise her statue in pure gold.
>
> .   .   .   .
>
> CAPULET. As rich shall Romeo's by his lady's lie,
> Poor sacrifices of our enmity.

With equal offers and clasped hands, the parents enact the spousal agreement between families that should have preceded the marriage of the young lovers, were it not for the feud. As the momentarily widowed wife of Romeo, Juliet will have from the Montagues a golden jointure equal to the golden dowry she brings from the Capulets.

The secret wedding in the tragedy raises other generally unrecognized issues concerning Paris's courtship of Juliet. Though in the play's immediate source he does not appear until after Romeo's banishment, from the first act Shakespeare shows this suitor following the route of conventional wooing. However, when Capulet agrees to the match, he abrogates the requirement for obtaining his daughter's consent, not even allowing a perfunctory interview between the couple. Juliet protests the breach of custom: "I wonder at this haste, that I must wed / Ere he that should be husband comes to woo." During the following scene, Friar Laurence expresses reservations to Paris about the girl's free assent, observing, "You say you do not know the lady's mind? / Uneven is the course. I like it not." Juliet's possible coercion, which would constitute an impediment to the marriage, is precisely the problem Paris addresses when she arrives at the friar's cell. Before a clerical witness, he tries to elicit her consent.

> PARIS. Happily met, my lady and my wife.
> JULIET. That may be, sir, when I may be a wife.
> PARIS. That "may be" must be, love, on Thursday next.
> JULIET. What must be shall be.
> FRIAR LAURENCE.   That's a certain text.
> PARIS. Come you to make confession to this father?
> JULIET. To answer that, I should confess to you.
> PARIS. Do not deny to him that you love me.
> JULIET. I will confess to you that I love him.
> PARIS. So will ye, I am sure, that you love me.
>
> .   .   .   .
> Juliet, on Thursday early will I rouse ye.
> *(Kissing her)* Till then, adieu, and keep this holy kiss.

Though she has deftly parried each statement, Juliet's parting kiss means, to Paris, an acceptance of their betrothal. Instead, as both she and Friar Laurence well know, the spousal is not valid because of her prior marriage to Romeo. The Nurse may rationalize, "Your first is dead, or 'twere as good he were / As living hence and you no use of him," and advise, "I think it best you married with the County." But any such union would be bigamy. This dilemma, which provokes Juliet's desperate solution, stems from the fact that Shakespeare has taken care to delineate a secret marriage satisfying religious and civil law in every respect.

The Recurring Image of the Inert Body in *Romeo and Juliet*

Brian Gibbons

The inert, either lifeless or lifeless-appearing, human body is a recurring image in Shakespeare's tragedies and *Romeo and Juliet* is no exception. Did the playwright intend these bodies merely as props necessary to or resulting from plot twists, or as powerful visual images conveying feelings and ideas? According to Brian Gibbons, a professor of English literature at the University of Münster, Shakespeare used inert bodies both as props and as images to evoke feelings and express ideas. As Riess and Williams do (see p. 78) in their essay about Pyramus and Thisby, Gibbons here refers to Arthur Golding's translation of Ovid's retelling of the Greek myths. Gibbons singles out the story of Pygmalion and draws a parallel between the sculptor's adoration of the statue he has created and Romeo's worship of Juliet's apparently lifeless body in the tomb. Just as the statue in the myth ends up coming to life, Gibbons points out, Juliet eventually wakes up, symbolically moving from a nonliving to a living state.

A silent and inert body may be alive, it may indeed be soundly sleeping, though it may also be unconscious, dreaming or dying. It may resemble in its beauty sculpted stone or it may be distorted and broken. A silent and inert body may be a dead thing, a corpse, the processes of corruption already at work within it, its humans identity disappearing.

The silent and inert body is a sign both of renewal and extinction: it is as powerful as it is ambivalent, a focal image of Shakespeare's dramatic imagination. He returned to it repeatedly in many different forms, though it is particularly intriguing to notice that it is centrally significant in his early non-dramatic work—the narrative poem *The Rape of Lucrece*.

Drama is a performance art in which the set codes and patterns are expressed with the direct immediacy of the actors' live bodies: the instinctive life of the flesh becomes part of a premeditated symbolic language, yet that premeditated code is at the same time risked in the existential circumstances of live performance. Paradoxically, it is when the body is silent and inert in a play that its contrasting aspects—of corporeal presence, sign for a person in the fiction, and intermittent symbolic-sculptural image—may be most apparent, as in *Romeo and Juliet* when Juliet lies in the Capulet tomb, near Tybalt's body in its bloody shroud, or—a less obvious case—in *King Lear*, when the blind Gloucester lies ominously still, having leapt from an imaginary cliff, and his apprehensive son Edgar kneels to examine him.

Shakespeare exploits the ambivalent potential of the actor's silent and inert body in stage performance, read or misread either as living or dead, and if dead as monument or corpse; he is also much interested in representing the body as undergoing transformation. I wish to concentrate on instances where Shakespeare endows the human body on stage with a further significance beyond its biographical status in the dramatic fiction—suggesting visually symbolic images analogous to sculpture. . . .

Even though they are non-verbal, these effects are necessary parts of Shakespeare's full theatrical language, integral rather than optional. The point needs emphasis since much debate among critics, designers and directors continues to focus on intermittently transmitted visual signs in Shakespeare. Such visual signs depend for their effect upon an audience being alerted in advance so that a particular code may be recognised, and sometimes theatre directors, actors and visual designers are insensitive enough to interfere with such signals. . . .

JULIET, A PRECIOUS STONE

In the discussion that follows I shall be concerned, in the first section, with Shakespeare's exploration of the ambivalences of the body, read or misread either as living or dead and, if dead, as monument or corpse, sacred or abhorrent; then, in the second section, I shall discuss his presentation of the body in transformation and transfiguration, recalling more directly the Pygmalion myth which contains the fundamental antinomies [contradictions]; but I begin with a play in which both issues are equally important, *Romeo and Juliet.*

In *Romeo and Juliet* at the beginning of the play the audience only hear talk of Romeo's beloved: she is a name, Rosaline, a subject of idealising poetry. In contrast, the first young woman the audience actually see in the flesh appears directly when her name, Juliet, is spoken. She is then made the subject of the Nurse's comic story, told in her presence, which vividly recounts details of her infancy—of how she was weaned from the breast at the age of three, when she 'could have run and waddled all about,' of how she fell and got a bump on her brow as big as a young cockerel's stone. The next time she is on stage she is dancing with others at the Capulet feast. Romeo sees her for the first time, falls for her, and transforms her into a metaphysical conceit:

> It seems she hangs upon the cheek of night
> As a rich jewel in an Ethiop's ear.

Here the quick, warm, dancing girl before his eyes is transformed into carved, anonymous stillness, precious stone. The same ambivalence plays upon their first kiss at the feast. The kiss is a stage image, a love-icon; at the same time it is a spontaneous physical event, an act in time. Its existential freshness transforms verbal quibbles on 'hands' and 'lips' and 'saints'. Yet Shakespeare has provided the audience in advance with a knowledge of Juliet not as a perfect erotic image but as a young girl at home with other women, amid talk of babies, toddlers, mild bawdy, and Susan (Susan and she 'were of an age') who died in childhood.

DEATH ASSOCIATED WITH SLEEP

As the play's narrative develops, Shakespeare marks its progress with a series of visible images of Juliet, love-icons from poetry transferred to the stage and embodied; but they are rendered ambivalent in the process. Juliet appears at her window overlooking the dark orchard, after the feast, and Romeo seeing her from below turns Juliet into a Petrarchan conceit 'It is the east and Juliet is the sun!" Yet Juliet is anxiously preoccupied at this very moment with what to do next in the real city of Verona where names cannot be wished away. In 4.3 the figure of Juliet being prepared as a bride poignantly evokes an image of ideal fulfillment, but the occasion (marriage to Paris) is in bitter contrast to the scene.

There are two details, however, which constitute a cinematic 'flash-forward': the bridal figure has by her a vial of potion and a dagger. Juliet's speech draws the audience's attention to the uncertainty of the potion's effect. 'What if it be a poison', she pointedly asks. 'I fear it is', she says. The doubt is focused on the curtained bed which remains in view after

ROMEO IN THE TOMB

In his death speech (from act 5, scene 3), Romeo beholds both Juliet's apparently lifeless body and the actually lifeless body of her cousin, Tybalt.

How oft when men are at the point of death
Have they been merry! which their keepers call
A lightning before death. O, how may I
Call this a lightning? O my love! my wife!
Death, that hath sucked the honey of thy breath,
Hath had no power yet upon thy beauty.
Thou art not conquered. Beauty's ensign yet
Is crimson in thy lips and in thy cheeks,
And death's pale flag is not advanced there.
Tybalt, liest thou there in thy bloody sheet?
0, what more favor can I do to thee
Than with that hand that cut thy youth in twain
To sunder his that was thine enemy?
Forgive me, cousin! Ah, dear Juliet,
Why art thou yet so fair? Shall I believe
That unsubstantial Death is amorous,
And that the lean abhorred monster keeps
Thee here in dark to be his paramour?
For fear of that I still will stay with thee
And never from this palace of dim night
Depart again. Here, here will I remain
With worms that are thy chambermaids. O, here
Will I set up my everlasting rest
And shake the yoke of inauspicious stars
From this world-wearied flesh. Eyes, look your last!
Arms, take your last embrace! and, lips, O you
The doors of breath, seal with a righteous kiss
A dateless bargain to engrossing death!
Come, bitter conduct; come, unsavory guide!
Thou desperate pilot, now at once run on
The dashing rocks thy seasick weary bark!
Here's to my love! [*Drinks.*] O true apothecary!
Thy drugs are quick. Thus with a kiss I die.   *Falls.*

Juliet drinks the potion and falls. Shakespeare keeps the audience in suspense during the ensuing scenes: the Nurse discovers Juliet: 'What, dress'd, and in your clothes, and down again?' Her father examines the body:

> Out alas, she's cold,
> Her blood is settled, and her joints are stiff.

When Romeo enters the tomb in the final scene he inspects her still body with intense attention; he has been told she is dead:

> beauty's ensign yet
> Is crimson in thy lips and in thy cheeks.
> And death's pale flag is not advanced there.

Then Romeo recognises another body lying nearby:

> Tybalt, liest thou there in thy bloody sheet?

A trick of the mind chooses 'sheet' not 'shroud', associating the bodies with sleep; at the same time the putrefying corpse of Tybalt gruesomely asserts itself, and perhaps deflects attention from those signs in Juliet which show her to be indeed mortal, that is, alive, though suspended so close to death. The state is one to which Shakespeare returns, evidently fascinated by its strangeness and mystery, as well as by its effects on onlookers. Instinctive taboos surround the body at the point of death. Romeo does not live to learn that he is deceived by Juliet's body. Even the lover steeped in passionate physical adoration cannot know his beloved's body well enough. Its transformations mystify and deceive even him.

HER SCULPTURAL STILLNESS AN ILLUSION

Golding's translation of the Pygmalion story from Ovid's *Metamorphoses,* Book 10 tells how an artist, Pygmalion, uses his imagination and 'wondrous' art to make a life-size sculpture of a young woman out of ivory. Golding's vocabulary insists on the ambiguity of the life-like work of art. Its eyes are closed, as if asleep or dead, a 'counterfeited corpse', yet it is an artefact so life-like that the sculptor himself cannot resist touching it—imagining it to be flesh—or kissing it—imagining his kisses are returned, even though his senses still tell him that it remains ivory. Then, a greater wonder: Venus herself intervenes, and as Pygmalion kisses the statue, this time the ivory waxes soft, and 'He felt it very flesh indeed'.

At the close of *Romeo and Juliet* the Pygmalion motif is handled with a deceptiveness foreshadowing Shakespeare's most paradoxical late manner. When Romeo breaks into the tomb to gaze on the body of Juliet, he is struck by the contrast of her unsullied beauty to the bloody corpse of Tybalt, lying nearby. Fleshly beauty as perfect as sculpture lies beside gruesome putrefaction. Right up to the last moment, poignantly, Juliet's sheer life-like beauty fills him with wonder: 'Ah, dear Juliet, / Why art thou yet so fair?' He will not pause to consider his own question, being convinced that Juliet is dead—and the audience themselves, though they know more than he does, cannot be sure whether she is unconscious or actually dead.

As it will turn out, Juliet's sculptural stillness is an illusion (she is about to wake up), and it is only in Romeo's dying speech that her physical beauty is miraculously immune to mortal decay. Like Pygmalion kissing his statue, Romeo kisses Juliet, but here in order to join her in death. Like Pygmalion's statue too, but again ironically, Juliet does wake up directly after the kiss—but by pure coincidence, not because of it. She finds Romeo dead (poignantly, she finds his lips still warm). She stabs herself, exulting in the thought of how swiftly Romeo's hardened steel will rust in her heart:

> O happy dagger,
> This is thy sheath *(stabs herself);* there rust, and let me die.

By one final paradoxical reversal, Juliet restores the Pygmalion myth while inverting it, dying 'with a restorative'.

The body always carries death within it, and in Shakespeare, where the body's pulse is so present to the dramatist's imagination, the possibility of its arrest must be so too. There is a certain feeling of awe associated with stillness, with inert and silent figures, in Shakespeare. It is partly that they aspire towards the ideal, the divine, beyond life. At the same time there is often a feeling of distaste, of recoil, since these still figures are associated with, insist on, our own death. Romeo's instinctive reaction against the corpse of Tybalt . . . finds an answer in every spectator.

The Influence of Astrology

John W. Draper

In this essay, taken from his book *Stratford to Dogberry: Studies in Shakespeare's Earlier Plays*, scholar
John Draper answers the frequent complaint of critics that "fortune" and "chance" play too important a
part in the unfolding events of *Romeo and Juliet*.
Draper argues that what is often interpreted as mere
chance is really part of a complex system of references to astrology, the supposed influence of the
heavenly bodies on human personality and behavior.
Astrology was widely accepted as fact in the Middle
Ages and Renaissance (and is still accepted today by
large numbers of people). In particular, Draper examines references in the play to the four "humors"
(or humours)—blood, phlegm, choler (or bile), and
black bile—the bodily fluids thought to help shape
human personalities, each humor being associated,
via heavenly influences, with certain days and times
of the day. Thus, the hot-tempered and vengeful
young Tybalt is seen as having too much choler, a
humor associated with fire, youth, and hot summer;
and his death at Romeo's hands takes place on Monday afternoon, a day and time when choleric powers
were thought to be weak.

Romeo and Juliet seems a tissue of improbable coincidence:
Capulet's illiterate servant happens by mere chance to ask
Romeo to read the list of those invited to his master's entertainment; Romeo, by a most unusual chance, decides to attend his arch-enemies' festivities, and so chances to fall in
love with Juliet; at just this time, the Prince chances to make
a stringent edict against brawling, and Romeo chances to
kill Tybalt and so is banished; and, also at just this time, Old

Excerpt from "Shakespeare's 'Star-Crossed Lovers,'" in *Stratford to Dogberry: Studies
in Shakespeare's Earlier Plays* by John W. Draper; ©1961 by the University of Pittsburgh Press. Reprinted by permission of the University of Pittsburgh Press.

Capulet chances to betroth Juliet to the Count Paris. Any one of these chances might singly be accepted; but why should they all occur within two days and just in the right order to set the plot in motion? Even more a matter of fortuity is the catastrophe: by chance, the Friar's letter to Romeo miscarries; by chance, Romeo meets and kills Paris at the tomb; by chance, the Friar is too late to intercept Romeo; and, by chance, Juliet awakens just too late to save her lover's life and just too soon for her father to save her from suicide. Indeed, never was love-affair more perfectly ill-timed; and yet, as if to emphasize this very fault, the master-dramatist, more than in any other play, marks, scene by scene, the days of the week and sometimes the very hours of the day. Truly . . . mere accident seems to guide the order of events; and, if this be so, the play has no integration of plot, does not illustrate the inevitable working of any general truth, and so can have no theme; without a theme, it has no ethos or significance; and, for all the gorgeous trappings of Shakespeare's lyric style, it is not tragedy but mere melodrama.

DOES FORTUNE AND CHANCE DRIVE THE PLAY?

Indeed, the critics have had difficulty in assigning to *Romeo and Juliet* any universal meaning. . . . Most critics, despite the obvious predominance of coincidence, seem to feel that the play has some sort of system or governing purpose; and they accordingly assign it various vague and rather divergent themes, none of which closely fits the plot or explains its sudden leaps without causality from one episode to another. Shakespeare generally gave the stories that he used a timely realism . . . and his utter failure to link the events of *Romeo and Juliet* in any certain, or even probable, connection is a strange departure from his usual artistry.

In the main trend of the story Shakespeare follows rather closely Brooke's poem, which is generally recognized as the chief source for the play. Brooke tells the tale as a "wofull chance," with little effort to explain the chances that occur; and he and [William] Paynter [author of *The Palace of Pleasure* (1567)], Shakespeare's other possible source, agree in repeatedly ascribing the course of events to "Fortune" or "false Fortune." Shakespeare, however, makes little reference to Fortune as governing the action; and these references appear too late to explain the motivation of the plot. A few passages somewhat casually ascribe the direction of events to "God" or "heaven"; but the play has no clear-cut Christian moral, unless it be the evils of brawling, as indeed Paynter suggests, or the wickedness of a secret marriage, as Brooke implies; and the catastrophe is not the inevitable consequence of either of these things. Nevertheless, over the play hangs a certain tragic fate. Juliet cryptically answers Paris, "What must shall be"; and reiterated [repeated] premonitions suggest an evil end: the Prologue refers to the "death-mark'd love" of the two protagonists; Lady Capulet, the Nurse, and Friar Lawrence give voice to ominous predictions; Romeo twice dreams—the second time that his lady found him dead; both lovers are "pale" and melancholy at parting; Romeo, even while arranging his marriage, casts his defiance at "love-devouring death"; he says that the killing of Mercutio "but begins the woe"; and he declares that he and Paris are "writ in sour misfortune's book." Juliet compares her love to the dangerous speed of lightning; her "all-divining soul" sees Romeo "As one dead in the bottom of a tomb"; she describes her case as "past hope, past cure, past help"; and, as she takes the potion, "a faint cold fear" as to the outcome "thrills" her veins. Is all this only . . . a mere pious pretence of inevitable catastrophe where no inevitability exists? Is Shakespeare no more than a theatrical charlatan, or did he really see in this tissue of circumstance a *rationelle* and motivation that is not clear to us?

PUPPETS OF THE STARS

Not only is the play replete with ominous predictions, but many of these predictions are associated with the hours and days and with the heavenly bodies that mark time. The Prologue refers to Romeo and Juliet as "star-crossed lovers." At the very beginning of the action, when Romeo starts for the Capulet feast, he says:

> . . . my mind misgives
> Some consequence, yet hanging in the stars,
> Shall bitterly begin his [its] fearful date
> With this night's revels, and expire the term
> Of a despised life closed in my breast,
> By some vile forfeit of untimely death . . .

In Act II, Friar Lawrence invokes the good will of "the heavens," but he fears that "after-hours will chide" all those concerned in the marriage. When Capulet forces Juliet to the unwelcome match with Paris, she cries out: "Is there no pity sitting in the clouds . . ." and later, "Alack, alack, that heaven should practise stratagems" against her. At Juliet's seeming death, Lady Capulet and the Nurse blame the day and hour as "Accurst" and "black" and "lamentable," as if the very calendar were responsible; and the Friar, even more clearly, imputes the misfortunes of Capulet to astral influence:

The heavens do lour upon you for some ill;
Move them no more by crossing their high will.

In Act V, when Romeo learns of Juliet's supposed death, he cries aloud, "then I defy you, stars!" And when he is resolved to kill himself, he says that death will "shake the yoke of inauspicious stars From this world-wearied flesh." Friar Lawrence imputes the killing of Paris to "an unkind hour," as if the blame lay on the heavenly bodies that mark the passing time. Thus, if Shakespeare meant what his characters seem to say, astral influence actually governs the lives of these "star-cross'd lovers"; and . . . they are the puppets of the stars and planets and of the days and times of day.

Although the stricter theologians looked askance and a few astronomers . . . must have had doubts, nevertheless the sixteenth century generally accepted astrology as a science: Queen Elizabeth regularly employed the learned Dr. Dee to compute for her the lucky days and hours for undertaking her affairs; and, though only specialists mastered the more esoteric mysteries of casting a horoscope, yet all classes devoured books of popular astrology, edition on edition, so that Ben Jonson could make it the basis of his masque, *Mercury Vindicated.* Everyone knew that the moon governed the rise and fall of tides; and what was man that he should escape such power? Indeed, the farmer had to know the changes of the moon for the planting of his crops; and almanacs, which supplied this astrological information, were so plentifully produced that the Lambeth Palace Library, for the year of 1595 alone, has no less than six by as many different publishers. Shakespeare himself makes constant reference to astrology. . . .

THE FOUR HUMOURS

To the Elizabethans, astrology had come down with some accreations from its Babylonian origins. They knew Greek astrology. . . . Indeed, the Greeks . . . had linked astrology with their other learning; and the result, as transmitted by the Middle Ages, was an integrated and complex theory that

AN ALTERNATE VIEW OF ASTROLOGY

This excerpt from the Treatise Against Astrology, *by Italian Renaissance scholar and humanist Pico della Mirandola (1463–1494), is a pertinent example of the extreme minority opinion of premodern times, one that both Shakespeare's audiences and the characters in* Romeo and Juliet *would have rejected.*

Astrology offers no help in discovering what a man should do and what avoid. . . .

Another use may be attributed to astrology: namely that it enables us to do whatever the astrologer advises and avoid that which he prohibits. I shall show that this [opinion] is either superfluous or harmful. The astrologer's predictions deal with matters of man's body or with external and contingent events. Turning to the first: supposing they concern health, we may ask whether his judgment agrees with that of a physician or differs greatly from it. If they both agree, the astrologer does nothing that the doctor could not do alone; if they disagree, which of the two, we may well enquire, deserves greater confidence? Surely, if a man ignores his doctor and entrusts himself to his astrologer, he deserves the penalty of his folly. Similarly, with respect to actions, the question is: does common prudence support whatever advice astrology may offer, or does its judgment go strictly the other way? If they agree, why seek among the far heavens what we can find at home; if they disagree, how can one defend as right and rational an action which in the process would ignore prudence—that prudence which, after all, amounts only to right reason applied to the doing of things?

An example will make this clear. Suppose an astrologer tells you that Mars will be very hostile to you, that with the power which his annual revolution provides he will raise your bile; that therefore you should use cold things and regulate your life against the heat of Mars. He tells you this from his reading of the skies; and the symptoms of your body, on which doctors rely in their diagnosis, either will or will not demonstrate the same. If they do demonstrate it, that will suffice to make you take precautions against future ill health. If they do not— if there is no sign of overheated bile but instead you have traces of albumen and fat in your urine, a sluggish pulse, pale complexion, weariness of the limbs, and all the other symptoms from which medical men deduce a preponderance of phlegm, not of bile—would you nevertheless think it right to evacuate bile because some astrologer pretends that Mars threatens you from the skies?

embraced and co-related physical and biological knowledge. Human beings were divided into four types, depending on which "humour," or bodily fluid dominated their physique; and each of these humours was associated with a certain day, with certain planets and constellations, with a chemical "element," a season of the year, a period of a man's life, a colour, a metal, and a bodily condition of heat or dryness. . . .

Perfect health of mind and body arose from a perfect balance of the four "humours" [blood, phlegm, choler, and black bile]; but, in most men, one humour or another predominated, either by nature from birth or by the circumstances of the occasion. Blood, supposed to be generated in the stomach, gave to those whom it controlled a sanguine temper; it was considered hot and moist and was associated with youth and springtime. Sanguine persons were thought to be under the influence of the constellations Gemini, Libra, and Acquarius, and of the planet Jupiter, and so were of a jovial disposition. This disposition especially prevailed from midnight to six in the morning, and its day was Thursday. Its colour was white, its metal electrum, and its chemical element the air. The sanguine man was handsome and lucky, and Jupiter was called "the greater fortune." A superfluity of phlegm, supposed to be genera'ed in the liver or perhaps the stomach, made a man easy-going, slow-witted and "phlegmatic"; this humour was cold and moist and moderately fortunate, and was associated with the element water, with women and children, and with autumn; such persons were under the influence of the constellations Cancer, Scorpio, and Pisces, and under either the planet Venus, which was grouped with Friday, copper, and yellow, or the moon, which was grouped with Monday and silver. The phlegmatic humour achieved its greatest power from six in the evening until midnight, and especially on Mondays. A superfluity of bile, called "choler," generated in the heart and found chiefly in the gall bladder, made a man wrathful or "choleric"; this humour was hot and dry, and was associated with fire, youth, and summer; such persons were presumed to be under the influence of Aries, Sagittarius, and especially Leo, and of the ill-omened planet Mars, whose day was Tuesday, or, more luckily, of the sun, whose day was Sunday; their hours were from six in the morning until noon, their metal was gold, and their colour red. A superfluity of black bile, generated chiefly in the brain and found chiefly in the spleen, made a man melancholy; this humour was cold and dry, and was associated with winter and old age; such persons were under the influence of Taurus, Virgo, and Capricorn, and of that ill-omened planet Saturn, and were therefore of saturnine disposition; their metal was lead, their colour grey, and their chemical element the earth. The present study proposes to examine the chief characters of the play to ascertain how well they fit into these four types, and how well their actions and the outcome of these actions accord with their days and times of day.

THE HUMOURS OF THREE YOUNG MEN CONTRASTED

Note the sharp contrast between Tybalt, Benvolio, and Mercutio. . . . Upon close examination, [this contrast] seems to spring from the fact that each represents a distinct type in the medical and astro-biological theory of the day. Tybalt is clearly of the choleric or wrathful type: he is always ready to fight, a quality that brings about the tragic catastrophe; he is "fiery" and "furious" and admits his "wilful choler"; and Benvolio refers to "the unruly spleen of Tybalt deaf to peace.". . . Of Tybalt's personal appearance, Shakespeare gives no direct clue; but certainly the timing and the outcome of the events in which he participates agree with the dominant hours of the choleric man: Capulet manages to quiet him at the festivities when Romeo appears; for it is between 6 P. M. and midnight in the phlegmatic period of the day; and Tybalt's fight and death on Monday afternoon are quite correctly timed: the day itself was phlegmatic and the time of day melancholy, and consequently his martial powers would have ebbed at noon, when the choleric part of the day was over. . . .

Also choleric, perhaps by nature, perhaps because of the season of the year, is Old Capulet. His wife, quite properly, thinks this humour inappropriate to his age; and, when in the first street-brawl he demands his sword, she suggests that a crutch would be more fitting. He is "too hot," *i.e.* too angry, toward Juliet; and his impetuous, headstrong nature, like that of Tybalt, directly contributes toward the tragic catastrophe. . . .

In sharp contrast to these choleric types is the phlegmatic Benvolio; and Shakespeare points and repoints this contrast. As Benvolio's name suggests, he is easy-going and friendly. "Fleame" was thought to be cold and moist and "wearyish";

and Benvolio is "weary." Such men were supposed to be affable, slow, dull, forgetful, soft of flesh, of small appetite, fat, short, possessed of little hair, of pale complexion, and given to dreams of rain and swimming. . . . Heat was supposed to make persons of this temperament more sanguine; and perhaps this influence makes Benvolio hopeful of avoiding brawls and, at the beginning of the play, of curing Romeo's love-sickness; but the heavens prevent his purposes; and, as the momentum of the tragedy develops, he drops out of sight, like the Fool in *Lear,* as if his phlegmatic temper and sanguine hopes and lucky influence were inappropriate to the catastrophe.

The name Mercutio, which Shakespeare derived from his source, doubtless suggested that the character be depicted as of the mercurial cast; and, indeed, this may have supplied the hint from which Shakespeare conceived his whole astrological tragedy. The mercurial temper is most difficult to define; for persons under that planet's influence might by attraction partake of any one of the four humours, and so were chameleon-like in their variety. . . . Just so, Mercutio changes to the wrathful type at the entrance of the angry Tybalt; and this same quick adaptability he urges vainly upon Romeo. The Mercurial man was supposed to be a "nimble person" and a go-between in love-affairs; and Mercutio by nature has "dancing shoes with nimble soles" and he joins with Benvolio in trying to distract Romeo and cure him of the unhappy love for Rosaline. This type, moreover, was supposed to be "volatile, sprightly, and ready-witted." Both Brooke and Paynter agree in calling Mercutio "pleasant and courteous" and popular with ladies; and they add that he had a fiery mind but cold hands—a suggestion of the inconsistent mercurial temperament. Shakespeare's Mercutio is certainly garrulous: he "talks of nothing"; he "loves to hear himself talk"; and he "will speak more in a minute than he will stand to in a month"; and, on occasion, he takes the stage for forty-two lines on the "inconstant" topic of dreams. . . . He is quite fitly killed on Monday afternoon—a phlegmatic day and a melancholy time of day that would depress the mercurial temperament and subject him the more easily to Tybalt's onslaught.

Juliet's old Nurse should also, perhaps, be accounted of the mercurial type. Juliet, to be sure, impatiently accused her of having the phlegmatic and melancholy symptoms of old age, "unwieldy, slow, heavy and pale as lead"; but, at the time, she is doubtless under the phlegmatic influence of Monday, and certainly her interminable garrulity and her willingness to shift from Paris to Romeo and back suggest that by nature she shares Mercutio's cast of mind. These minor characters, especially Tybalt and Mercutio, conform rather closely to their astrological prototypes; and an examination from this point of view of the two principals in the play would seem to be worth making.

JULIET PASSIONATE, ROMEO COMPLEX

Juliet is clearly of a hot, passionate temperament. She falls in love with Romeo at first sight, and she even dares to gainsay her father's orders to his face. The Nurse calls her "hot" and tells an anecdote of her babyhood that the credulous might interpret as a sign of passion. At the beginning of the play, she is not quite yet fourteen, and so has hardly had an opportunity to show her nature; but the stars had given her this nature even from her birth, and Shakespeare carefully impresses on the audience the horoscope of her nativity; and twice we are told that she was born on "Lammas-eve at night," that is when the sun was in the house of the constellation Leo. Those born under Leo were supposed to be choleric and passionate if not incontinent, inclined to be stout and often barren; and the type was associated with youth and summer. If then Juliet is of this hot complexion, her planet should be Mars or the sun; and with the latter the text constantly associates her: she shines so brightly that she shames the torches; she is called the "sun"; Romeo refers to her "light"; Friar Lawrence compares her to "the sun" clearing away Romeo's sighs; Juliet herself compares her love-thoughts to "the sun's beams"; she is a "lantern" and "her beauty makes This vault a feasting presence full of light"; and, at her death, the Prince declares that "The sun for sorrow will not show his head.". . . Some of these references may be mere metaphor, but they are too numerous and too apt to Juliet's choleric nature to be entirely accident; and, moreover, metaphor was so commonly a part of the method of scientific thought that a metaphoric use does not preclude a strictly technical one. Juliet, therefore, like Tybalt and Old Capulet, is hot and dry, but only moderately so, for she is under the influence of the sun rather than of Mars. . . .

The most complex of all these figures is Romeo. He first appears as an example of the melancholy type, and so suffers under the influence of Saturn, which was styled "the greatest infortune." Even before he enters, his father describes his tears and sighs, and declares that his "humour" is "black and portentous." He has been avoiding the sun, and "locks fair daylight out"; and, when he enters, he declares that the love for Rosaline that afflicts him is a "choking gall." Clearly, Romeo, whatever his natural humour, is suffering from love-melancholy. Heaviness and the metal lead were particularly associated with this bodily condition; and Romeo is "heavy"; he "cannot bound a pitch above dull woe"; he has "a soul of lead"; and he compares his love to a "heavy lightness" and a "feather of lead.". . .

On falling in love with Juliet, however, Romeo rebounds to his natural self. Melancholy is cold and dry, unhappy, and saturnine; but Romeo, in the bloom of youth and lofty station, could partake of such a humour only because of some immediate, overpowering impulse, for "Trouble and affection" can change one's disposition. Romeo, by nature sanguine, quickly returns to his innate merry self. Indeed, at the very moment that he climbs Juliet's garden wall, he would seem to renounce his former bitter mood: earth, as a chemical element, was associated with melancholy; and Romeo cries out: "Turn back, dull earth, and find thy centre out." This tendency to variable extremes was in itself a sign of a hot disposition; for such a humour was described as "variable and changeable."

In the last four acts, Romeo clearly shows the effects of his sanguine humour. His whole love affair betrays a cast of mind that is hopeful against obstacles, and impatient of cold reason; and this very quality helps to induce the tragic ending. Even as he leaves Juliet, condemned to exile from Verona, he is still hopeful, and protests against "Dry sorrow" because it "drinks our blood"; and he prosecutes his wooing and insists upon the marriage, with an untimely haste. . . . Romeo's sanguine humour, moreover, fits with his good looks: the Nurse catalogues his physical attractions . . . in the best sonnet style. . . . Truly, he seems to show all the good qualities of the sanguine man. He has also the weakness of the humour: blood could produce "riot and wilfulness"; and those who had a superfluity, when "too much chafed," are prone to act "like mad-men"; quite of this sort is Romeo's rage against Tybalt, and his rage against himself when he has killed Tybalt, "The unreasoning fury of a beast." In short, Romeo, in his rapid changes from saturnine love-melancholy to his natural joyous disposition, and then on occasion to unreasoning rage, is a rather clear portrayal of the sanguine man: he woos Juliet in one night and marries her next day in defiance of all obstacles; he has the sanguine man's good looks and wit and dignity of bearing, and also his wilful fury under provocation. The choleric Tybalt, Capulet, and Montague, all under the influence of Mars, the choleric Juliet under the influence of Venus, the phlegmatic Benvolio, the mercurial Mercutio and the Nurse, and the sanguine Romeo, now under the power of love-melancholy and now of fury: all of these surely make of *Romeo and Juliet* an astrological tragedy of humours.

CHAPTER 3

Diverse Ways of Staging and Interpreting *Romeo and Juliet*

How the Lovers' Scenes Were Staged in Elizabethan Times

Leslie Thomson

Shakespearean scholars vigorously debate his plays' original staging. One frequent focus is the structure of the typical Elizabethan stage, particularly the back wall, behind which was located the "tiring house," where the actors dressed and kept their costumes and props. Apparently, parts of the tiring rooms were sometimes used in staging the plays; when curtains were drawn (or part of the back wall was removed) an alcove-like space, sometimes referred to as a discovery space, became a staging area for crucial scenes.

In this essay, Leslie Thomson, a teacher at Erindale College, University of Toronto, suggests how this discovery space and other parts of the stage may have been used specifically by Shakespeare and his contemporaries in staging the important scenes between the title characters in *Romeo and Juliet*. Thomson devotes particular attention to the climactic tomb scene, making the point that the tomb and Juliet's previously seen bedchamber may have occupied the same space on the stage; and she further suggests that Shakespeare used highly descriptive wordplay to emphasize the relationship between these settings already hinted at visually in the staging. Thomson calls the transformation of the bedchamber into the tomb a "metamorphosis of bed to bier."

The stage for which Shakespeare wrote, with its medieval heritage and physical equivalents of heaven, earth and hell, invited the integration of the visual and verbal for thematic purposes. At the same time, the staging conditions imposed particular demands on the playwright, requirements which

From "'With Patient Ears Attend': *Romeo and Juliet* on the Elizabethan Stage" by Leslie Thomson, *Studies in Philology*, vol. 92, no. 2, Spring 1995. Copyright ©1995 by the University of North Carolina Press. Used by permission of the publisher.

are accommodated, even capitalized on in the play's setting and dialogue. A play that seems especially worth exploring with this in mind is *Romeo and Juliet,* since at several points when the staging is particularly complex the language becomes vividly descriptive, helping the audience to imagine what would have been difficult to see. In the absence of pictorial evidence, we cannot know how certain kinds of action were staged or settings represented, and examples of what are perhaps the most problematic kinds of scene—window, bed and tomb—all occur in this early Shakespeare play. The focus here will be the relationship between what the characters say and what they do in these interrelated scenes, since it seems likely that the one is intended to describe the other for the practical reason that the staging would have necessitated it. More particularly, I should like to join those who have speculated about the staging of the tomb scene by considering not only how the scene is prepared for both verbally and visually, but also how and why the language of the scene itself describes the action. At certain points in *Romeo and Juliet,* perhaps what the characters say was determined as much by the circumstances and conventions of staging as by the themes, because the stage was used to emblematize [symbolize] those themes.

CREATING VISUAL IMAGES

The dialogue descriptions of the setting and action in 5.3 [the tomb scene] are so specific and often seem so literal that, on the one hand, one is tempted to posit the use of a "discovery space" or enclosure of some sort even if such a staging would have limited the ability of many spectators to see the action of this and several other key scenes. Conversely, one might argue that the detailed verbal pictures were intended to take the place of real sets and large props. Theatre historians, textual critics, and editors have advanced a variety of differing opinions about how such scenes were staged, but in general these can be divided into three camps. The still predominant view is that the stage for which Shakespeare and his contemporaries wrote had a discovery space in the tiring house wall where study, tomb, shop, and perhaps bed scenes were located. As well, there are those who have persuasively argued for a specially built structure jutting out from the tiring house wall for such scenes, particularly in plays which also have upper level action. Finally, there is

... [the] "minimalist" view that more often than not no special staging was required for such "enclosed" scenes, which were performed forward on the main stage itself.

Regardless of which staging one favors—and it remains largely a matter of conjecture and opinion—none would completely eliminate visibility problems inherent in the requirements of the plot and action of *Romeo and Juliet.* I therefore suggest that Shakespeare, having in mind the stage(s) on which the play would be performed, capitalized on the physical conditions to create thematic visual images; and that a necessary function of the dialogue was to introduce, describe, confirm, or embellish what the audience saw. This idea is implied at the conclusion to the Prologue's summary of the "two houres trafficque of our Stage. / The which if you with patient eares attend, / What heare shall misse, our toyle shall striue to mend." There are different versions of 5.3 (especially Romeo's speech), in the first (1597) and second (1599) quartos. Most textual critics agree that Q2 is likely closer to what Shakespeare wrote, and with the "false starts" deleted Q2 is the copy-text for modern editions, with apparent clues about the staging added from Q1, which seems to have the authority of performance. Studies of Arthur Brooke's *The Tragicall Historye of Romeus and Juliet* reveal that as always Shakespeare adapted his source to suit his purposes, sometimes virtually repeating Brooke, sometimes departing from the poem substantially. But while he did not slavishly follow Brooke, Shakespeare, like his source, set the death scene of Romeo and Juliet in the Capulet tomb. This may seem almost inevitable, but it also raises problems since on the page the scene needs only description, but on the stage is rather more complicated, perhaps requiring a semi-enclosed location, certainly seeming to demand verbal embellishment for dramatic effectiveness. This being so, it is I suggest hardly coincidental that Romeo's speech in the "tomb": describes what he does as he does it; tells the audience to whom he is speaking; expresses his thoughts; and, in so doing, gathers together at the play's climax its visual and verbal motifs.

OXYMORONS AND OTHER WORDPLAY

As many critics have noted, this play contains a number of poetic conventions.... Focus on the language has perhaps obscured the simultaneous use of staging conventions, but the two—verbal and visual—are complementary, something made especially apparent when the play is considered in the context of its original performance space(s). Along with the poetic conventions, the language of *Romeo and Juliet* is characterized by several related devices, the most pervasive being wordplay in general—puns and double entendres abound. Of particular importance is the use of oxymorons: juxtaposed opposites with thematic implications controlling what the audience both sees and hears. In addition, there is repetition—linguistic, structural and physical—making the specific devices more apparent. Together these emphasize the interrelationship of love and hate, marriage and death, sweet and bitter, light and dark, high and low.... In *Romeo and Juliet* the oxymorons are made visual by Shakespeare's use of the physical properties and conventions of the Elizabethan stage.

The extant evidence indicates that in the London theatres at least there would have been a stage platform and an upper gallery, however minimal, probably with a corresponding space beneath it, behind the tiring house wall. While many plays do not require use of the tiring house space above or below, and most of those which do could be performed on a provincial or great-hall stage with neither, *Romeo and Juliet* is not one of these. The source(s) Shakespeare was adapting virtually required the use of both levels, the theatrical result being that in this play the physical relationship between stage and gallery is thematic as well. Furthermore, the use of a bed in Act 4, closely followed by the bier in Act 5 would have invited the spectators to perceive thematic connections in the transition from room to tomb. Thus when first Romeo and then Juliet die in the Capulet tomb the paradox-resolving transcendence suggested by the language and imagery would have been conveyed visually by the staging as well.

Both thematically and theatrically the tomb scene is the last of a related series in which Shakespeare uses the playing space to convey the lovers' progress through the play. Based both on what the dialogue tells us and what we know or guess about the Elizabethan stage, in 2.2 Juliet is above, Romeo below; in 3.5 both are above and Romeo descends. Then in 4.3 and 4.4 Juliet is on her bed, which probably would have been "thrust out" from the tiring house; finally, in 5.3 Romeo breaks into the tomb—perhaps the discovery space (where the medieval hell-mouth would have been?), perhaps a thrust forward prop, perhaps a specially built or portable structure. These scenes thus visually chart the inexorable downward movement of the action: the fate of love in a world of hate. And in each scene the dialogue helps the audience to see, both literally and figuratively.

FROM GALLERY TO BEDROOM SCENES

At the start of the first gallery scene (2.1), Romeo focuses the audience's attention on the appearance of Juliet above: "what light through yonder window breaks?" He then describes her actions: "She speakes, yet she saies nothing"; "See how she leanes her cheeke vpon her hand." As this scene between the lovers progresses, Shakespeare seems to prepare for the tomb scene while at the same time giving the audience a clear visual impression. Juliet asks how Romeo has come there, since "The Orchard walls are high and hard to climbe, / And the place death, considering who thou art." The romantic Romeo replies, "With loues light wings did I orepearch these walls, / For stonie limits cannot hold loue out." These last words can apply as well to his later breaking into the tomb—calling attention to the two visible, analogous violations of sacred, Capulet, space which anticipate then complete the unseen act of consummation....

In the second gallery scene (3.5), the opening aubade makes explicit—indeed, directs—the movement of Romeo away from Juliet: "Wilt thou be gone? ... I must be gone and liue, or stay and die.... Therefore stay yet, thou needst not to be gone." When Romeo then says he will risk death and stay, their roles reverse: "Come, death, and welcome," says Romeo; "hie hence be gone away," pleads Juliet. Finally they describe their physical separation. *Juliet:* "Then window let day in, and let life out." *Romeo:* "Farewell, farewell, one kisse and Ile descend." *Juliet:* Art thou gone so? loue, Lord, my husband, friend." When Romeo has descended—presumably via the rope ladder suspended from the gallery—Shakespeare gives Juliet a speech which: establishes the staging; probably brings her to lean over the balustrade, making her more visible; and graphically anticipates the final scene.... After Juliet descends to join her mother, the ensuing confrontation between parents and daughter is played out on the main stage, which has now become her bed chamber, in thematically and theatrically significant language. As if to signal the downward movement, Lady Capulet angrily exclaims, "I would the foole were married to her graue," and by the end of the Act, Juliet is alienated and alone, prophetically rhyming "remedie" and "die" in this play where paradoxes are resolved and words echo into deeds. . . .

BED BECOMES BIER

After Juliet is told she must marry Paris, she goes to her bed chamber and prepares to simulate her death. In its staging and language this scene (4.3) clearly anticipates the later one in the tomb; as well, it makes visual the already voiced conflation of bed and bier. Unlike Romeo in the tomb, Juliet is alone in this scene; but like Romeo's later speech, her soliloquy is explicitly descriptive of her actions—actions an audience would probably have had difficulty seeing since as she speaks Juliet would likely be first near and finally on her bed, which, although probably "thrust out," would have been equipped with canopy and curtains restricting visibility. . . .

Most of the rest of Juliet's soliloquy is concerned with her fearful imaginings of waking in the tomb. Besides introducing heavy proleptic irony [showing something or introducing an idea before its proper time], the vivid descriptions serve the practical purpose of creating the tomb in the mind's eye of the spectator even before the scene which takes place there. This is especially effective, even necessary, if in 5.3 there would be little for the audience to actually see because of either or both limited staging possibilities and restricted visibility. The speech ends when Juliet, imagining she sees Tybalt's ghost seeking Romeo, drinks the potion. . . . The action-describing words suggest that the oxymoronic ceremony of marriage-in-death has begun here, to be completed in the tomb by first Romeo, then Juliet. Furthering this idea, Q1 ends the scene with the stage direction, "*She fals upon her bed within the Curtaines.*" Juliet's long speech here, in which she vividly imagines the tomb and Tybalt's ghost, combined with the lamentations of the others immediately following, are preparation for her later death—in fact, Juliet is as good as dead from this point in the action. If Juliet's bed was in the same location as the tomb, the foreshadowing would have been visual as well. Certainly, when it comes Juliet's final short speech in 5.3 completes and affirms what is enacted here.

When the Nurse enters to awaken Juliet, the focus of the action is once more the curtain-enclosed bed. The Nurse's speech is very like Romeo's later in the tomb: she speaks to another who cannot hear, and describes more than an audience can see. As the Capulets, Paris, and the Friar enter, the dialogue implies that they go to the bed to see the dead Juliet for themselves. . . . Regardless of whether the bed was located within a recess in the tiring house wall below the

---

ELIZABETHAN STAGES

Shakespearean scholar Charles Sisson offers this brief overview (quoted from A Companion to Shakespeare Studies*) of the structure of a typical Elizabethan theater stage.*

[The] main outlines of the Shakespearian stage are clear enough, though there will always be obscure points of detail open to conjecture and debate. . . . There was a raised stage jutting out into a 'yard' or pit. The audience stood in the pit into which it projected, or sat in the galleries built around the theatre walls and fronting the stage. A few even purchased stools on the stage itself or sat on the rushes with which it was strewed. One gallery was, as it were, continued behind the stage, which it probably overhung, and to which it formed an adjunct as an upper stage. Behind the stage were the tiring-rooms of the actors, in which they dressed and kept their properties, costumes and play-books, from which they emerged upon the stage and into which they entered upon their exits. In the wall of the stage, which was hung with arras or tapestry, were three openings, one door on each side, and a larger opening in the centre curtained off and revealing, when the curtain was drawn, a space behind the stage, being part of the tiring-room area. This space furnished a second adjunct to the main stage, an inner stage. All three openings were at the back of the stage and communicated with the tiring-rooms, which were built in three stories, so that the upper stage could be entered directly from them, as well as from the front by occasional scaling-ladders. An active man could, indeed, safely jump down from it on to the main stage. Over the whole stage-structure projected the 'heavens' or canopy, also accessible apparently from the third-story tiring-room. It stood upon posts resting on the stage and protected it from the weather. The spectators' galleries were roofed, but the pit or yard was open to the sky. Finally, the tiring-rooms communicated also with the space underneath the stage, which was boarded off, in communication with trap-doors constructed in the stage-floor, which afforded a further means of entrance and exit.

gallery, or in a specially built semi-enclosed space (with a playing area above it) forward of the tiring house, or was thrust out from the tiring house, the actor on/within it would have been difficult for a spectator to see.

The Q1 direction for the curtains to be shut at the end of the bed chamber scene makes it possible to speculate that the bed was not pushed back into a tiring house recess but remained on stage with its curtains closed until the tomb scene, only 160 lines later, when Romeo finds Juliet dead. Not only the conventions of the unlocalized stage, but staging practicality would seem to dictate a verbal—and visual— metamorphosis of bed into bier. Certainly the intervening dialogue helps to create just such a transition, or duality. When Balthasar tells Romeo that Juliet's "body sleepes in *Capels* monument," Romeo vows "Well *Juliet,* I will lie with thee to night.". . .

PREPARING THE AUDIENCE FOR WHAT IS TO COME

[In the tomb scene] what has previously been Juliet's bed and bed chamber, the pervasive verbal oxymorons take physical form most clearly. . . . The fictional chamber above where Romeo and Juliet have consummated their marriage has, by degrees, become the tomb below where the ceremony will be completed. The "light" of Juliet—of love—seen by Romeo through her window in 2.1 now illuminates the tomb for him—and, metaphorically, for the audience.

Having fulfilled Paris's dying request, Romeo shifts his attention to Juliet. His words, besides being ironic reminders to the audience that Juliet is not dead, are also a practical necessity since they describe what no theatre audience can really see, regardless of the staging. . . . Because the verbal emphasis is on Romeo's perception of Juliet and a spectator's ability to see her is almost inevitably restricted, the audience's knowledge that she is alive is set against Romeo's belief that she is dead but does not "yet" show it. Furthermore, Romeo, "a dead man," speaks to his "dead" wife before the adjectives are true—"too early" in the context of the action, but right on time dramatically and thematically, as the language gradually prepares the audience for what is to come.

Having again anticipated the lovers' deaths, Shakespeare has Romeo briefly shift his attention to the dead Tybalt and once more the speech is also a description of action not easily seen. Note how it is voiced as questions, which act as reminders that those to whom Romeo speaks cannot answer, and why:

> *Tybalt* lyest thou there in thy bloudie sheet?
> O what more fauour can I do to thee,
> Then with that hand that cut thy youth in twaine,
> To sunder his that was thine enemie
> Forgiue me Couzen. Ah deare *Juliet*
> Why art thou yet so faire?

By placing Romeo's address to Tybalt between his words to Juliet, Shakespeare makes explicit the relationship between love and hate which has governed the play and brought Romeo Montague to the Capulet tomb to die. . . .

LOVE TRIUMPHS OVER DEATH

If Romeo's last speech is as much description of staging and action as thematic rumination, nowhere is this more apparent than at its conclusion—when the important business of an actor bending over a reclining body would be difficult to see. . . . Romeo's last line ["Thus with a kiss I die."], often celebrated for its oxymoron-resolving wordplay, is also a detailed description of action. At this crucial thematic moment Shakespeare leaves little to chance by inviting an actor to "suit the action to the word, the word to the action.". . .

With Romeo's and Juliet's deaths the movement of the two lovers through the play is complete. Critical discussion of their final speeches often focuses on how the language of love, life, and marriage—the elements of comedy—is used by the protagonists to describe their deaths—events of tragedy. As noted, this essentially theatrical conflict—words contradicting actions—has been prepared for from the play's first moments by the numerous oxymorons. But if the opposites of wedding bed and bier are to be understood by the audience as key signifiers of a finally resolved whole, this scene in the tomb will direct that perception. And the specific quality of the resolution, conveyed by what the lovers say, is a product of the relationship between, on the one hand, the necessities and conventions of Elizabethan staging, and, on the other, Brooke's poem with its description of the tomb scene and emphasis on Fortune.

Although Romeo believes he is acting in defiance of the "stars" and being his own "pilot," his actions at the end are determined from the start—when his love for Juliet in a world of hate places him on Fortune's wheel, making the downward motion inevitable.... Romeo's "pilgrimage" to the Capulet monument to join his wife in the tomb as he has in the bed chamber is an affirmation of the power of love over hate. As both the visual bed-bier conflation and the sexual puns of their dying speeches suggest, the two transcend the world that has destroyed them. At his end Romeo might say, "The wheel is come full circle. I am here" [a famous line from Shakespeare's *King Lear*] ... in affirmation and triumph. The language of Romeo and Juliet in the tomb tells us that for them the bitter is sweet, the darkness, light. An audience saddened by the lovers' deaths is prompted not only to accept their inevitability but also to see Romeo and Juliet as having risen metaphorically above the world of competing, inanimate statues they leave behind. In the terms of the medieval concepts that linger behind the play's language and staging, Love triumphs over Fortune and Death.

Shakespeare Used Extensive Character Doubling in Staging *Romeo and Juliet*

Giorgio Melchiori

One of the most common practices in Elizabethan play staging was character doubling; that is, having one actor play two or more different characters in the same performance. Such doubling, useful not only to avoid the expense of hiring extra actors to play very small roles, but also in the event of a shortage of qualified actors, became an art form in the hands of the best writer-managers of the day. Shakespearean scholar Giorgio Melchiori here contends that doubling was used extensively in the original production of *Romeo and Juliet*. Part of the evidence, he says, lies in the early printed editions of the play, the First and Second Quartos (designated Q1 and Q2), which contain various handwritten stage directions; these notes not only offer clues to how Shakespeare and his colleagues conceived the staging, but even sometimes refer to certain roles being taken by specific actors in Shakespeare's company, including the popular comics Will Kempe and John Sincklo and the tragedian Richard Burbage. Melchiori offers an insightful and convincing argument for who doubled whom and the resulting effects on the play's staging.

The definition of *Romeo and Juliet* as a tragedy has always been challenged on the grounds of the casual nature of the *dénouement* [final resolution of the plot]. Critics have felt bound to qualify the definition by calling it 'the tragedy of chance', or a love comedy with a tragic ending ... [or] a lyrical tragedy, the counterpart of the lyrical comedy that Shake-

From "Peter, Balthasar, and Shakespeare's Art of Doubling" by Giorgio Melchiori, *Modern Language Review*, October 1983. Reprinted by permission of the author and the *Modern Language Review*.

speare was creating in the same years in *Love's Labour's Lost.*

It is perhaps at first sight surprising that in a play like this, keyed to the language and the conventions of courtly love poetry, the roles of the servants are developed to an extent which is hardly reached even in the lightest comedies: fifteen per cent of the words in the play are spoken by servants. Of course the Nurse accounts for a large part of it, but in the versions of the story known to Shakespeare her part was much more limited; and Balthasar, Peter, Sampson, and the rest of the Capulet servingmen who turn up at all stages of the play are largely Shakespeare's own additions. The introduction of these characters, together with those of the critical involved observer Mercutio and of Romeo's confidant Benvolio, is Shakespeare's way of making theatrically effective the lyrical mood in which the play was conceived. . . .

I propose to focus on two of the servant characters, who seem to have intrigued editors and critics. . . . They are Peter, the Nurse's escort, and Balthasar, Romeo's man. I believe that a close study of these two characters can serve . . . to throw light on Shakespeare's practice of doubling. . . .

THE CLOWN AND OTHER SERVANTS

The Capulets' servants are, one and all, given to broad jokes and low wit. Peter makes a brief appearance, as a mute, in II. v, promptly sent out by the Nurse ('Peter stay at the gate'). The next witty Capulet servant to turn up is in IV. ii, when old Capulet is frantically organizing Juliet's wedding feast. His order, 'So many guests invite as here are writ, Sirrah, go hire me twentie cunning Cookes' (there is no need to believe, as many editors do, that these are orders addressed to different servants), elicits a couple of typically clownish replies from the servingman. His lines, in prose like Peter's and Sampson's, suggest that they were intended for the same actor—why add to the number of speaking parts, since they were all servingmen of the house of Capulet? On the other hand Capulet's first words seem to be a deliberate echo of the order he had given to another unnamed servant in I. ii. 35, 'Go sirrah trudge about | Through faire *Verona,* find those persons out, | Whose names are written there', an order that resulted in the comic meeting of the illiterate servant, unable to read the list, with Benvolio and Romeo, and the latter's attendance at the Capulets' ball and meeting with Juliet. In this case we have the evidence of Q2 that Shakespeare had cast this servant as the clown, since his stage-direction at the beginning of I. ii reads *'Enter* Capulet, *Countie* Paris, *and the Clowne'* (though the word *clown* might mean simply a rough and illiterate person, the use of the definite article probably points to a specific theatrical role). In their turn the reporters of Q1 bear witness, with their stage-direction, *'Enter Clowne',* that it is a clown, or should we say *the* Clown, who comes in at the end of the next scene to call Lady Capulet, the Nurse, and Juliet: 'The guests are come, supper serv'd up, you cald, my young Lady askt for, the Nurse curst in the Pantrie, and everie thing in extremitie.' And again the same actor comes forth with napkins and orders other servingmen about shortly after, at the beginning of I. v, addressing them in exactly the same breathless style: 'You are lookt for, and cald for, askt for, and sought for in the great chamber'. It may be significant that this character is the only one designated in Q2 with the speech-heading *'Ser.',* while the other servingmen here are simply 1, 2, and 3.

Verbal and stylistic links make it clear that Shakespeare was well aware of the necessity of doubling, and deliberately wrote the parts of the different servingmen in such a way that the same actor, and a favourite one with the audience, could play most of them. Actually, when he did not want yet another servingman to be impersonated by the clown, he made this quite clear. At IV. iv. 13, after Capulet had dispatched the clown with the list of guests and told him to look for cooks ... it would have been awkward to have the same man come on stage again in the pursuit of further domestic chores. Significantly in Q2 (reflecting presumably Shakespeare's own manuscript), not even the word *servingman* is used (as in IV. ii); the stage-direction reads *'Enter three or foure with spits and logs, and Baskets',* and the speech-heading is *'Fel.'* for 'fellow'; and to make doubly sure that the clown is not one of the 'three or four', Capulet is made to say 'Call *Peter,* he will shew thee where they [drier logs] are', to which one of the 'fellows' replies 'I have a head sir that will find out logs, | And never trouble *Peter* for the matter'.

PARTS WRITTEN FOR WILL KEMP?

It could be maintained that all these precautions against an awkward doubling were taken in view of the final entrance of the clown a hundred lines later in the same scene ... after the choral dirge for Juliet's apparent death. It is just at that point, however, that a major difficulty arises: Q2 has the stage-direction *'Exit omnes'*, as if the scene and the act should most appropriately close at this point; but this is immediately followed by the extraordinary further stage-direction *'Enter Will Kemp'*, introducing the comic scene between the clown and the musicians. The obvious suggestion is that this part of the scene is a later addition for the benefit of the most popular clown of the time, who was also, until 1599, a sharer in the company of the Chamberlain's Men. . . . The very mention of the name of the actor seems to imply that when Shakespeare first wrote the play he had in mind no particular actor for the different short comic roles; only when Kemp joined the company, probably in 1594, was the clown's role extended and he (or somebody else) jotted down his name. . . .

The implication is that *Romeo and Juliet*, or most of it, was originally written before 1594, and such dating is consistent . . . with the characteristic features that distinguish this play from all the other tragedies, *Titus Andronicus* included. It looks as if, for once, Shakespeare was writing without having in mind specific actors. . . .

I am suggesting that Shakespeare started writing *Romeo and Juliet* at a time when the situation of the theatres in England was very uncertain and there were even doubts about the possibility of their survival. I am referring of course to the years 1592–93, for most of which the London theatres were closed because of the plague as well as for political reasons; established companies disintegrated, merged, or moved to the provinces, and the plague took a heavy toll of the actors themselves. It is generally accepted that in view of this situation Shakespeare turned in those years to the writing of narrative poems that would secure him the patronage of the cultured aristocracy, and *Venus and Adonis* and *The Rape of Lucrece*, published in 1593 and 1594 respectively, were the result. . . . He was no longer sure who would act the play [*Romeo and Juliet*] or even whether it would appear at all on the public stage. He thought that the most likely audience for it might be just those noblemen whose patronage he was seeking in writing his poems; hence the adoption of the lyrical style of courtly love poetry. . . .

If we accept this reconstruction of the writing of the play, we can see that the first four acts, up to IV. v. 95, were written with no definite idea of who should play the clown in his different reincarnations as Sampson in I. i, the servingman sent on the errand of inviting the guests in I. ii, the other servingman who comes on in I. iii and I. v and again in IV. ii, and finally Peter, the Nurse's man. All these bit-parts strung together were still not enough for such a popular actor as William Kemp, so his final scene with the musicians was added. . . .

Whoever added the scene between the clown and the musicians (why not Kemp himself?) was familiar with the previous impersonations of the clown in the play. His punning boast to the musicians, 'I will cary no Crochets, ile re you, Ile fa | You, do you note me?', is an appropriately musical variant of the very first line of the play, the clownish Sampson's boast 'weele not carrie Coles', which unleashes another torrent of puns on 'collier', 'choler', and 'collar'. Will Kemp was doubling all the parts of the clownish servants of the Capulets that I have listed above, from Sampson to Capulet's personal messenger, from the butler who calls the ladies to the feast and orders about the other house-servants, to Peter, the Nurse's escort.

THEIR ABSENCE MORE SIGNIFICANT THAN THEIR PRESENCE

Why, it could be asked, all this doubling and these different names if the audience would recognize one and the same actor in the various impersonations, the more so since all of them used the same tricks of language and of manner and wore the same livery of the house of Capulet? The explanation lies in the complex hierarchical distinctions among the servants of the great Elizabethan families. Sampson and Gregory, in I. i, are obviously in the top bracket, the equivalent of today's bodyguards of the most prominent members of the family; they would therefore carry a sword or a rapier to come to the rescue of their masters as well as a dagger for personal defence (Benvolio in fact shouts to the servants on both sides, 'put up your swords', at I. i. 61). Peter, as the personal servant of a mere dependent of the household, would not be authorized to carry a sword, but only a dagger: such is the 'weapon' he mentions at II. iv. 155, and waves in jocular threat at the musicians in IV. v. 121 (the Second Musician replies: 'Pray you put up your dagger, and put out your wit'). The servants employed in strictly domestic duties or sent round on private errands . . . would wear no weapon at all. Such distinctions were so rigid and so generally accepted that it would have been improper to call all of them by the same name, though it was also accepted that their physical appearance, their language, and their behaviour should be identical, and therefore that on the stage one clown could impersonate them all. . . .

Romeo and Juliet is a play that requires a good deal of doubling. . . . There are some forty speaking roles in the play, nineteen of which have more than four speeches or 140 words each. It is well known that the average Elizabethan company had no more than a dozen players (sharers and half-sharers), plus some boys and hired men, up to a maximum total of eighteen. Discussing 'The Number of Actors in Shakespeare's Early Plays', [Shakespearean scholar] William Ringler, Jr, has shown that no more than sixteen are required for any of the plays written up to 1599. . . . Now, the final tableau of *Romeo and Juliet* requires the presence on stage at the same time of practically the whole company, since there are at least thirteen identified characters with speaking parts, plus as many extras as could be mustered as attendants of the Prince and of the Capulets and Montagues (Q1 directs *'Enter Prince with others'*).

The absence of some major characters in this all-on-stage scene (as well as in the other crowd scene of the play, I. v) is more significant than their presence, because it suggests that the actors taking their parts are needed to impersonate other minor figures. Mercutio and Tybalt have of course been dead since III. i, and may have taken over any of the secondary parts; I shall come back to Tybalt in a later section of this paper. At first sight the handsome and courtly Benvolio, also strangely absent in v. iii, might appear a likely 'double' of Paris, but the doubling Paris-Benvolio is made impossible by I. ii, where Benvolio comes on stage at line 45, only seven lines (that is to say, hardly one minute) after the exit of Paris at line 37. Also Peter and the Nurse are absent from the last scene of the play; the two of course go together, and, apart from the fact that there is no scope for clowning at this stage for Peter (the clown could at most take over the part of one of the muddling watchmen), the Nurse, obviously a mature actor and not a boy, may well have been doubling a male character of some consequence. The likeliest is old Montague, who appears in only three scenes in the play, the very first, the last, and the middle one (III. i), from all of which the Nurse is absent; actually, after his exit at the end of III. i, the long and not strictly necessary monologue of Juliet gives the actor ample time to change back from Montague into Nurse.

WHAT HAPPENED TO BENVOLIO?

Even less justified than that of the Nurse is the absence of two other characters from the last scene of the play: Lady Montague and Benvolio. In the case of Lady Montague the author felt so strongly the need for a justification that he decided to kill her off, in contrast with the sources; coming on stage at line 209, the first thing that Montague says is: 'Alas my liege, my wife is dead to night.' The boy taking the part of Lady Montague was probably required as Paris's page. It is a different matter in the case of Benvolio: he had been the one close confidant of Romeo from the very beginning of the play (though he did not appear in the source story), an extremely serviceable dramatic invention to 'feed' the hero's display of mood and feeling, to act as mediator between him and the audience and as objective narrator at key moments of the play; it is surprising that he should disappear after his report to the Prince on Mercutio's and Tybalt's death in III. i (a report ending with the line 'This is the truth, or let *Benvolio* die'), and that he should not be present at his friend's death and at the reconciliation between the two families which he had always tried to promote. . . .

What had happened to the actor who had been playing Benvolio, a longish serious role (1160 words, sixty-three speeches nearly all in verse)? For which other role was he required in the last part of the play, so that he could not appear again as Benvolio? I am going to suggest that the same actor doubled the roles of Benvolio and Balthasar, and that this was Shakespeare's intention from the moment he was faced with the necessity of presenting on the stage Romeo's man (even before deciding on his name) to bring in the news of Juliet's apparent death and to escort Romeo to Juliet's tomb. Romeo's man is in fact fulfilling in the last act (as he did incidentally in the source story) the role of confidant that had been Benvolio's in the first part of the play, and it is dramatically correct that the two characters with the same function should be identified with each other. Balthasar's part is sharply differentiated from those of all the clownish servingmen in the play, and it extends to 233 words (twelve speeches) all in verse; it requires an adult actor of a certain standing and capacity in both verse delivery and stage presence. A doubling with Peter, as I hinted at the beginning of this paper, is inconceivable: the audience would have immediately recognized, under the Montague livery of the servant entering at V. i. 11, the clown who had left the stage only a couple of minutes before as Peter at the close of IV. v, and their response would have been totally wrong. Instead, even if they recognized in the new character the same actor who had been Benvolio, another member of the Montague family, their expectation would have been perfectly fulfilled by the sedate poetic language of the new speaker. . . .

Modern editors have made the confusion worse by tampering with the stage-direction in I. i, at line 31. The second Quarto and the later seventeenth-century editions have *'Enter two other servingmen'*, while Q1 specifies: *'Enter two Servingmen of the Mountagues';* from the speech-headings it appears that one of these Montagues' men is called Abram while the other is a mute and is never given a name. In 1709 [the well-known poet and dramatist Nicholas] Rowe, determined to give a proper name to all the characters in Shakespeare's plays, and finding that the only other Montague servant named in the tragedy was Romeo's man, Balthasar, replaced the stage-direction with *'Enter Abraham and Balthasar'*, and most later editors followed suit. . . . Alas, the damage done by Rowe . . . [has] become irreversible: no modern producer, convinced of the presence on stage at the same time in I. i both of Benvolio and of Balthasar as a mute, could ever dream of casting the same actor for both parts, even if this meant increasing production costs by putting another full-time actor on the company's pay-roll.

This type of editorial zeal tends to obscure one of the great skills of Shakespeare as a playwright. In his hands the practice of doubling was an art. As a man of the theatre he was conscious that his plays would be acted by companies with a very limited personnel, and it was his job to allocate the roles in such a way that, whatever their number, they could all be played by just over a dozen speakers. He obviously did not bother with the very short parts, making single appearances in the course of the play; for instance in *Romeo and Juliet* any actor could have taken the role of the Apothecary (except those playing Romeo, Balthasar, and Friar Lawrence, the last entering immediately after the Apothecary's exit). Even if (as somebody suggested in view of the allusion to the extreme leanness of the character) Shakespeare was thinking of giving the part to that paragon of leanness, John Sincklo, it would not be the only part that such an experienced comedian (as distinct from the clown) would take in the play; Mercutio would be the most likely role for him, though it was not necessarily written with him in mind.

THE QUESTION OF PARIS'S DOUBLE

I must repeat that when Shakespeare started writing *Romeo and Juliet* it is very likely that the company of the Chamberlain's Men had not been formed yet, and he had no idea who was eventually going to perform the new play. So he could not think, as he certainly did when writing his later plays, in terms of specific roles for William Kemp, John Sincklo, or, for that matter, Richard Burbage. All he knew was that he must write a play suitable for a group of at most twelve main actors, and a few extras, either adults or boys. He knew as well that most of these actors would have to impersonate more than one character. So he had on the one hand to devise a strategy in the distribution of the parts that would allow for the necessary changes of costume between exits and entrances of the same actor in different roles, and on the other hand to arrange them in such a way that such doubling of parts would enrich and quicken rather than confuse the audience's response. Shakespeare's art of doubling is the actual creation of 'doubles': Sampson-Peter (and of course the other clownish servants of the Capulets) and Benvolio-Balthasar are examples of his ability to play variations not so much on stage-types as on certain dramatic functions and their incarnations as characters. In the first case the function played upon is that of the clown, in the second that of the hero's confidant. . . .

Romeo and Juliet, apart from the analogy of roles (the clown, the confidant), reveals subtler aspects of this use of doubling. The Prince who speaks the formal epilogue to the play must also have been cast as the Chorus, that is to say, the Prologue, since . . . the second chorus was hardly ever performed. He is in fact the objective narrator, in contrast with Friar Lawrence (another possible speaker of the prologue) who is instead a manipulator of the action, while Benvolio-Balthasar is a witness. But there is another and more striking possibility. Let us consider the character of County Paris, a comparatively small part, which implies that the actor taking it would be available to impersonate also other characters in the course of the play. In discussing V. iii I have explained why the doubling of Paris with Benvolio is impossible, even if the latter were not doubling Balthasar. . . .

Who, then, is Paris's double? The obvious approach to the question is through a consideration of those scenes where he does not appear, and since we have seen that the most crowded scenes are also the most revealing in the matter of doubling, we should turn in the first place to I. v, the ball at the house of the Capulets: a scene that, even more than those considered before, requires the presence on the stage of the whole company. County Paris had been pressingly invited to take part in the entertainment by Capulet himself, and Lady Capulet had assured Juliet that the young man, her prospective husband, would be present. So modern producers show us Paris dancing with Juliet in the background while Romeo watches, wondering at the beauty of the girl. When we turn to the original edition of the play we find absolutely no evidence of the presence of Paris in this scene; on the contrary, whatever evidence there is is positively against it. A study of the staging of the Capulets' ball . . . demonstrates this very extraordinary fact: Shakespeare has arranged things in such a way that it is impossible for the most expected guest to participate at the Capulet's feast, though an extremely able manipulation of the audience's expectations gives them the illusion that Paris is there. Why does Shakespeare play this sleight of hand on the audience? The reason, I feel sure, can be only one: because the actor impersonating Paris is present on the stage in I. v *in another role.* In other words, Paris cannot be present at the ball because he takes part in it as somebody else, somebody in fact very different. I suggest that one and the same actor doubled Paris and Tybalt. The two are never on the stage together, neither is any exit of the one close to the entrance of the other. Tybalt is the first to appear in I. i, but he leaves the stage at line 101 and the scene runs on for another 135 lines, so that there is all the time needed for the reappearance of the same actor as Paris at the beginning of I. ii. Tybalt figures on stage only twice more, in I. v and III. i, while we must wait until III. iv to see Paris again. It will be said that they are sharply contrasted characters, the one violent and boisterous, the other a gentle follower of the conventions of courtly love. But let us consider their specific dramatic functions in respect of Juliet: she hates neither of them, but they are each in turn the stumbling-blocks on the way to her union with Romeo. It is significant that Shakespeare, departing from his source story, makes not only Tybalt but also Paris die at the hands of Romeo. I am not suggesting that Paris's death is due to the fact that he was doubling Tybalt; rather I think that the recognition of the identity of the dramatic functions of the two characters prompted Shakespeare's idea both of having Paris killed by Romeo *and* of doubling the two parts. Such a piece of doubling would enrich the audience's response to the structure of the play and create an awareness of its implications.

The art of doubling has been lost for centuries, first through a preoccupation with naturalistic presentation, then through the taste for spectacular productions with large expensive casts. Only the last few decades have seen a return to the Elizabethan simplicity of staging, but producers, in order to achieve some savings in the actors' payrolls, have had recourse to ruthless cutting, eliminating all inessential minor parts. The point is that there are no inessential roles in a Shakespeare play. Now, at a time of economic crisis in the theatre, producers would be well advised to go back to Shakespeare's original texts, adopting his own devices to save manpower on stage. Doubling is much better than cutting, as it actually enhances a play's dramaturgic values. But generations of textual editors have disregarded this aspect of Shakespeare's art and are providing texts that require an absurdly large number of actors. They should instead pay greater attention to the indications of the original stage-directions and refrain from indiscriminate additions that (in their preoccupation with 'naturalistic' staging) obscure the author's intentions in respect of casting. By studying the possibilities of doubling implicit in Shakespeare's texts they would render a valuable service, not only to modern producers, but to Shakespeare's own art.

Editing the Play's Text

Barbara Hodgdon

Over the centuries, various stage and film directors have omitted lines, rearranged speeches and scenes, and otherwise edited Shakespeare's plays, including *Romeo and Juliet.* The director's rationale is usually that such editing is necessary to express a personal vision of the piece or to interpret the play in context of the time, place, and culture in which it is performed. But a number of people, ranging from literary and dramatic critics to ordinary playgoers, have objected to cutting speeches and scenes from the play's original text, suggesting that this editing alters the author's intentions. The critics often use such terms as "directorial interference in" or "actors' corruptions of" Shakespeare's "sacred" text. In the following essay from the prestigious *Theater Journal,* scholar and essayist Barbara Hodgdon argues that such critics have been far too harsh and that it is perfectly valid for directors to edit *Romeo and Juliet*'s text to fit the interpretation of a given performance. Citing examples from various renowned stage productions of the play, as well as director Franco Zeffirelli's 1968 film version, Hodgdon suggests that each director has the right to create his or her own "performance text" of the play, a concept, she points out, that Shakespeare himself would readily understand and validate.

From Juliet's death forward, *Romeo and Juliet* describes a series of seemingly anticlimactic events analogous to those in the final scene of a detective fiction: alarmed discoveries by the Watch, the Prince, and the lovers' parents; accusations; hurried questions; appeals to authority and patience; the Friar's lengthy explanation; the evidence of imperfect near-witnesses, Balthasar and Paris's Page; Romeo's letter to his

From "Absent Bodies, Present Voices: Performance Work and the Close of *Romeo and Juliet*'s Golden Story" by Barbara Hodgdon, *Theatre Journal*, vol. 41, no. 3, October 1989, pp. 341–59; ©1989, The Johns Hopkins University Press. Reprinted with permission of the publisher.

father, appropriated by the Prince just before he accuses the feuding families; the fathers' reconciliation, including their somewhat discomforting commercial rivalry over the golden statues; the Prince's conclusive pronouncement. Even though Shakespeare's playtext crowds multiple entrances and explanations together, repeating a pattern initiated by the other two crowd scenes, it seems almost perverse, especially in a play that calls attention to its characters' impatience and the speed of its events, for the action to slow down (once it's too late), to have and take all the time in the world to resolve its "two hours' traffic." Particularly at issue are the Friar's forty-one lines, retelling the story for the assembled community, asking for pardon. Following [the well-known eighteenth-century essayist] Samuel Johnson, who thought it "much to be lamented that the poet did not conclude the dialogue with the action, and avoid a narrative of events which the audience already knew," eighteenth- and nineteenth-century theatrical practice concentrated upon the lovers' deaths and then provided a symbolic tableau of reconciliation, constructing closure as a condensed image of the privileged lovers, one which . . . has persisted throughout theatrical history as an almost obligatory finale. Although he admitted that *Romeo and Juliet*'s ending lacks . . . "resourceful breadth of effect". . . [noted modern Shakespearean producer and critic] Harley Granville-Barker argued for restoring not just the Friar's speech but Shakespeare's full scene. Contemporary theatrical practice, however, pays only selective attention to his suggestion. Details of several recent stagings can provide a kind of composite map of this history of loss, restoration, and further loss.

THREE CONTRASTING VERSIONS OF THE FINAL SCENE

[Noted stage director] Peter Hall's 1961 Royal Shakespeare Company *Romeo and Juliet*, for example, offered fairly representative cuts. Hall compressed the Watchmen's dialogue and cut fourteen lines of the Friar's speech—including its somewhat contradictory opening, "I will be brief, for my short date of breath / Is not so long as is a tedious tale"—as well as the explanations of Balthasar and Paris's Page, moving directly from the Prince's "We still have known thee for a holy man" to "Where be these enemies?" and so on through to the conclusion of Shakespeare's text. Following the Prince's last lines, a mass exit generated the familiar stage picture of Romeo and Juliet's entwined bodies, positioned slightly off-center, their presences overwhelmed by the massive walls of the tomb. Slow drumbeats from offstage marked the growing distance between mourners and dead; finally, the single lantern, carelessly left behind, which had illuminated their faces, went out.

In 1976, Chris Dyer, [director] Trevor Nunn's designer, transformed the Royal Shakespeare Theatre into a Globe-like auditorium, with an open stage, the proscenium arch disguised, and two balcony rows of seats running across the back of the stage. Nunn's Romeo, Ian McKellen, carried Francesca Annis's Juliet from a midstage trap, let her stand, and then held her close, her arms encircling his neck as he sat, his feet in the tomb-trap on "Here will I remain." As he drank the potion, one of Juliet's hands fluttered with life, and Romeo fell, Juliet in his arms, just as her hand moved to touch his cheek. From this point forward, Nunn's staging played a nearly complete text, which concluded by recognizing the double function of the final speech as both narrative close and epilogue. Whereas the Prince spoke the first two lines, Chorus addressed the rest to the audience, splitting this last partial sonnet between two speakers as though to echo the sonnet Romeo and Juliet shared when they met at the Capulets' ball. And then, on this simulated Elizabethan stage, the play immediately dissolved as Chorus waved on the rest of the company for the usual bows. . . .

[By contrast, noted film director] Franco Zeffirelli's 1968 film of *Romeo* and *Juliet* [omitted] the discovery scene entirely . . . cut[ting] from the lovers [lying dead in the tomb] to a high-angle long shot of Verona's public square, seen through veils of early-morning mist. The Montagues and Capulets, who twice before exploded into this space in parallel intercut movements, now joined in single, solemn procession, bearing Romeo and Juliet's bodies, dressed in their wedding garments, to be buried. To the sounds of tolling funeral bells and torches sputtering in the wind, the mourners' footsteps echoed on the stones as the families gathered on the church steps. The camera isolated individual faces (especially the Nurse's), which reflected guilt, sorrow, and loss. Then, in a low-angle close-up, the Prince's "All are punished!" admonished both on-screen and off-screen watchers, equally complicit in the play's tragedy.

As the two families filed through the cathedral door toward the camera, a brief pan, from full shot to mid-close-up, isolated the dead lovers, side by side on the bier. Then the credits began to roll up: next, the film image was further enclosed with a lattice-like golden frame. Again, the camera singled out particular faces and groups. Intriguingly, the women remained separate, aloof and hesitant; it was the men who touched or embraced. Like Shakespeare's, Zeffirelli's Verona threw the weight of privilege to masculine power. The film's last shot held on Verona's massive walls, seen from the empty square, while Laurence Olivier's sonorously authoritative tones, in voice-over, spoke the story's epilogue. As in the film's opening shot, the sun was just rising, and if it seemed that Romeo and Juliet's story was over, with the Montague-Capulet feud resolved on a conciliatory note and the picture firmly set within an enclosural frame, it could also have seemed that this story is possibly, perhaps infinitely, repeating itself—just as the film, as cultural product, is infinitely repeatable, always the same.

Among these performance variants, Hall's finale typified not only the prevailing stress on the Prince's patriarchal authority but also the option of a kind of viewer's choice, which replaces one final stage picture—the familial reconciliation—with another—the spotlit image of the two lovers, abandoned by their parents—thereby offering spectators a last, painfully perfect, voyeuristic glimpse of timeless union. Like Hall's, Nunn's staging also "belongs" to Romeo and Juliet. Although splitting the Prince's speech with the Chorus blurs the distinctions between play and "after-play," between onstage and offstage communities, and thus joins stage and world, implicating both in the tragedy, the earlier moment when Juliet wakes almost in time to catch her Romeo generates a poignant emblem of haste and loss, captured in memory ... which seems to override these last emphases and to crystallize both the play's events and the spectator's experience. And ... Zeffirelli's finale ... with its satisfying circular return to beginnings—contains and encloses Shakespeare's tragedy within a fictional frame, distancing spectators from loss.

"TOO MUCH PRODUCTION AND TOO LITTLE PLAY"

Whereas each of these *Romeo and Juliet*s certainly invited spectators to recognize that loss, each also (though perhaps in varying degrees for particular spectators) memorialized the lovers' story . . . [permitting] individual spectators either to negotiate their own contemplative relationship to that story or, in the case of Zeffirelli's film, to assuage and subsume their responses within the final, amplified, and overly sentimental sequence of atonement. Two other *Romeo and Juliet*s, forty years apart, effected a more unsettling negotiation between Shakespeare's playtext and its audiences. For very different reasons, each constructed a sense of ending from textual absence; both constitute examples of my second, confrontational, model of *Romeo and Juliet's* performance history.

The time is 4 April 1947; the place, once again, Stratford-upon-Avon. In the week preceding the opening of [stage director] Peter Brook's *Romeo and Juliet,* the first Festival offering at The Memorial Theatre, press announcements touted the twenty-two-year-old director's revolutionary (at the time) decision to cast young unknowns, eighteen-year-old Daphne Slater and twenty-six-year-old Laurence Payne, in the title roles. Assured of violence and passion—Brook's tag-line for the production was "for now, these hot days, is the mad blood stirring"—and promised no sweetness or sentimentality but rather "a genuine Elizabethan spirit," the first-night audience gathered outside the theatre in the early April evening. . . .

Although Brook and his designer, Rolf Gérard, started with elaborate (and expensive) scenery, they began throwing it out at dress rehearsal, gradually reducing the stage to an empty hot-orange arena and a few sticks. Much later, Brook justified this decision by claiming that "[*Romeo and Juliet*] is a play of wide spaces, in which all scenery and decoration easily become an irrelevance, in which one tree on a bare stage can suggest the loneliness of a place of exile, one wall an entire house." But if for Brook . . . *Romeo and Juliet* offered a vehicle for exploring a stagecraft "which could give freedom and space to the sweep of the poem," his critics . . . condemned its reckless spectacle, "which sacrifices poetry, acting, and even the story itself, to pictorial splendor."

Brook's critics did not confine their objections to what one called "flashes of almost Technicolour vehemence" and another "too much production and too little play." Stratford's reared-on-Shakespeare audiences began to murmur when they failed to hear Benvolio's long speech about the

Mercutio-Tybalt-Romeo fight and the Friar's explanation of the potion's effects to Juliet—omissions that seemed especially odd.... And finally, as *The Times*'s reviewer noted, "Mr. Brook is so little interested in the characters that he omits altogether the reconciliation of the houses over the grave of the 'poor sacrifices of their enmity.'" These as well as other comments about the production's localized features finally crystallized into a generalized critique of failure. Brook's *Romeo and Juliet* lacked "the urgency of Shakespeare's rhetoric," "the high emotional requirements of the infinite tragedy," sacrificing "sentimentality and starshine" to the unfamiliar. "If to be lean and harsh, with glowing purple patches here and there," said the *Guardian*'s critic, "is also to be unmoving in the deeper sense, what happens to the famous claim of tragedy on our pity and terror?"...

Responding to criticism, Brook justified his choice by faulting Shakespeare as well as his company: the scene, he said, is "elongated [and] contains extremely clumsy writing ... we could not bring it to life." Curiously attuned to the playtext's own emphases on fate and chance, Brook's ending seems more like a hasty accident resulting from his own youthful frustration than a deliberately crafted, distinctive directorial innovation.

PLACING THE LOVERS IN AN IMAGINARY FUTURE

Nearly half a century following Brook's impulsive decision to drop Shakespeare's last scene on the rehearsal-room floor, the close of [director] Michael Bogdanov's 1986–87 *Romeo and Juliet*—one of the Royal Shakespeare Company's entries in the category of what some might call contemporary decorated Shakespeare—revealed a more purposefully radical erasure at work: 140 lines of Shakespeare's playtext absent; in their place were eight lines from the Chorus's opening sonnet, the tenses changed from present to past. Although only two of Brook's reviewers noted the absence of *Romeo and Juliet's* final scene, nearly every report of Bogdanov's version described, and sought to interpret, its use, or misuse, of Shakespeare's playtext. Briefly, let me reconstruct its dominant features.

As Juliet stabbed herself with Romeo's knife—"there rust, and let me die"—a blackout, accompanied by music (a signal that the play was not yet over), covered what was to be revealed as a spectacular transformation: when the lights came up, Romeo and Juliet stood on the tomb, their faces masked and bodies caped in shimmering golden fabric. Family members, friends, and bystanders—including several photographers—gathered around the statues as the Prince presided over their unveiling; he read a cut version of the first Chorus from two note cards. As he finished, more *papparazzi,* flashbulbs popping, rushed down the aisles to orchestrate posed pictures of the Mafioso Prince, the two fathers shaking hands, the two sets of parents, Friar Lawrence, the Nurse . . . and the drug dealer-apothecary, who had supplied Romeo with a foil-wrapped packet of, presumably, heroin for "cordial" injection. Once the moment was recorded, milked of its potential publicity value, the Prince swept off with his entourage, refusing further comment; the others left as well—some pursued by reporters, some ignored. Lady *Montague* (still living) placed a rose at the foot of Romeo's statue. Benvolio remained, seated down left at a cafe table. He rose, crossed toward the statues for a last look, and slowly walked away as the lights went down on the two figures, the final sign of what, much earlier—and speaking of Paris, not Romeo—Lady Capulet called "the golden story."

Whereas Shakespeare's close concerns discovering the true story behind the final melodramatic tableau of bodies, Bogdanov's finale constructed an ironic, near-parodic substitution for melodrama—by rewriting those bodies as the spectacle Shakespeare's playtext places in an imagined future and by fixing *Romeo and Juliet*'s story as different from that which spectators have seen and (presumably) been complicit with. Irving Wardle of the *Times* found this particular representation a harsh transformation of Shakespeare's "pious thought that the lovers' deaths have patched up the family feud [into] an irreconcilable clash between affection and property"; Benedict Nightingale of the *New Statesman* called it "a grotesque distortion of Shakespeare, who wanted to suggest that out of love, pain, death, good might come." For the critical community, Bogdanov's brashly unique collaborative endeavor, which used Shakespeare's playtext as a trampoline, broke through its textual envelope, and bounced into postmodern flight, simply was not *Romeo and Juliet* "as they liked it." Rather, appropriating Shakespeare's playtext to represent—and confront—contemporary cultural phenomena risked connections which, at best, critics described as unnecessary relevance, at worst, as anachronistic, transgressive violations of *Romeo and Juliet*'s presumably trans-historical meanings.

THE CONCEPT OF A "PERFORMANCE TEXT"

Bogdanov's finale illustrates several of the perceived threats contemporary performances represent: the reappropriation of textual elements; the potential enslavement of text by spectacle; the disappearance, destruction (as opposed to de-construction), and ultimate consumption of the text. . . .

Increasingly . . . contemporary textual scholarship sug-gests that the playtext itself is mutable, subject to change from its very inception. Several of Shakespeare's playtexts—*Hamlet* and *A Midsummer Night's Dream*—not only enact this mutability but even specifically authorize Elizabethan versions of what critics and scholars have called directorial interference and actors' corruptions, terms which assume an ownership over the written text not unlike that of overly pro-tective fathers preserving, from all the world, their daughters' chastity as a sign of their own patriarchal power. When the players come to Elsinore, Hamlet takes the First Player aside, "Can you play 'The Murder of Gonzago'? . . . You could for a need study a speech of some dozen or sixteen lines which I would set down and insert in't, could you not?" Hamlet tai-lors an extant text in order to make it "speak . . . with most miraculous organ" to a particular audience at a particular time, to represent his personal and political designs. . . .

Fortunately for dramatic history . . . William Shakespeare documented . . . Prince Hamlet's production concept and its intent. . . . But Bogdanov's final scene for *Romeo and Juliet,* with its minimal textual authority—eight reappropriated lines—belongs to another category—playing—which in Shakespeare's own time had primacy over "the play" as a printed object. Indeed, he wrote within and against a system of performed representations, which was at least as privi-leged, if not more so, than the published (literary) text of the play. Today, however, scholars tend to measure performances against a peculiarly obsessive brand of Shakespearean qual-ity control—the extent to which the performance successfully (or unsuccessfully) competes with the printed text or, more significantly, with each reader's private, ideal construction of that text, for authority. To some extent, such an attitude as-sumes that a Shakespearean playtext will not only speak for itself but that it will also (miraculously) ventriloquize and make accessible its past historical moment. Theatre history, however, suggests a more specific historicity for the representation of Elizabethan playtexts. Peter Brook, a director who claims no interest in history, only one in the aesthetic relations between performances and their audiences, posits, in a statement seemingly designed to protect his own work from history, the particularly ephemeral life of theatrical representations: "A production is only correct at the moment of its correctness, and only good at the moment of its success. In its beginning is its beginning, and in its end is its end." Reflecting on such representations as well as on Shakespeare's own practice invites considering Bogdanov's body play, as well as the other versions of *Romeo and Juliet*—for which I have admittedly provided less than complete descriptive maps—as *performance texts.*

Quite obviously, such a label seeks textual authority for theatrical representation. Here, what is first of all essential is to encounter the conceptual illusion behind the term "text." The very word appears inviolate, enclosed—an "x" or "nexus" fenced in by two powerful t's. Appropriating the term and coupling it with "performance" intentionally threatens both the notion of an established, authoritative written text of a Shakespearean play and the notion that those written words represent the only form in which a play can possess or participate in textuality. . . . Certainly the contemporary critical climate recognizes and gives value to the multiple, imperfect states of many Renaissance texts, challenges the notion of an inviolate canon, and generates renewed attention for the collaborative atmosphere which gave rise to theatrical representations. Why, then, not give equally privileged attention to radically imperfect and radically variable performance texts? . . .

To return, then, to Bogdanov's performance text and to interrogate its choices. In the strictest sense, his rewritten ending neither violated nor distorted "Shakespeare's text" (whatever that may be) at all. Rather, by leaping over those 140 lines, Bogdanov began after the playtext ended, in the white space following the written words, a space which invites inhabitation and representation. In choosing to reappropriate and truncate the opening Chorus at the close, Bogdanov was listening to, and reproducing, the broken sonnet that ends Shakespeare's own playtext. The use (or killing) of that sonnet not only enforced a confrontational connection between the beginning and ending of the original by rewriting ending as beginning but also invited rereading the story as a tabloid, late-night news-fiction, a commodity of scandal providing the occasion for a photographic opportunity. The Prince's central position and his indifferently casual reading from cue cards revealed how authority exploits such spectacle to reconstitute its power. . . . Rather than attempting to appropriate a missing past or recapture a lost reality, Bogdanov's close situated itself as an integral part of contemporary cultural production driven by images. . . . Here, the ideological purpose of spectacle was turned against itself, its parodic construction simultaneously enslaving those on stage and (potentially) empowering those in the audience.

THEATER INTERSECTING WITH SOCIETY

In the late 1980s, the intertextual connections between Bogdanov's performance text and our own social space have a weekly, if not daily, familiarity. The program for the production invited, even enforced, those connections. Rather than quoting a range of critical opinions on the play or providing background material on Elizabethan culture, that program reproduced excerpts from current cultural studies of love and marriage and suicide. This document, together with the poster, reviews, "thick descriptions" of the entire performance text, Bogdanov's prompt copy, a series of photographs taken at dress rehearsal (many of which were designed as star shots), and a videotape shot with a single camera equipped with a zoom lens, point the way toward an even larger notion of textuality. . . . To extend further the open or dispersed textuality of Bogdanov's performance text as a cultural event, it would be necessary to gather additional interview and biographical material from actors, director, and designers; descriptions of the rehearsal process; information on the economic circumstances of production; whatever critical perspectives figured in the shaping of the performance text; and the decodings of the production generated by particular interpretative communities—including hostile spectators.

This *bricolage* of discourses, this potential archive, constitutes not just the exclusive province of theatre historians but the foundation for a more global project of criticism, one which I call *performance work*. By this I mean the . . . theatre's ability to do cultural work—to trace, intersect with, and intervene in the dimensions of the social sphere. Such an enterprise requires that we rethink the compartmental, mutually exclusive formulations we apply to that floating entity we call "the play." It requires that we give up the conventional opposition between a so-called authoritative text and performance, find ways to negotiate contradictory worlds—Renaissance and postmodern—and permit those contradictions to energize rather than limit our discourse. It requires that we view theatrical representations not as fraudulent rites enacted by rival priests, rites where we mourn the loss of desired familiarity or signs of a glorious past, but as activities that participate in historical processes and in the ideological work of shaping present-day reality. Such performance work invites a redirected critical praxis—one which embraces Shakespeare's playtexts, their variant critical reformations, and performance texts in order to dance a new historical rag, a kind of present historicism . . . which addresses current cultural practice—so that what we now attempt to recuperate for Shakespeare's time we also do for our own. In evoking the absent bodies of a number of *Romeo and Juliet* performance texts, giving them a present voice, my own performance work writes a brief history of its close—a history which re-inscribes the playtext's own remembering, interpretation, and confrontation within a cultural framework and which attempts to re-imagine the theatre's ability to participate in the ideological work of giving varied shapes to our loss, endowing it with a "local habitation," offering us pardon—and, on occasion, naming us as the chief, though not the only, begetters of that loss.

A Film Version of the Play Uses Visual Imagery to Enhance the Story

Michael Pursell

> Film is a visual medium; therefore, a filmed version of a stage play can potentially be very effective in using visual imagery to convey the meaning and intent of the work. Often, such imagery can and does replace some lines and even whole scenes. The visuals, especially close-ups, which are impossible onstage, can also enhance the spectator's feelings for the characters and, overall, create a highly authentic atmosphere.

Michael Pursell, of the faculty of England's prestigious Nottingham University, here examines the use of such visual imagery in renowned director Franco Zeffirelli's highly acclaimed 1968 film version of *Romeo and Juliet.* Pursell maintains that Zeffirelli carefully strove for a blending of artifice, or a sense of the fictional and storybook qualities of the piece, and authenticity, a feeling that the events of the story are really happening before our eyes. By cleverly and effectively employing color-coordinated costumes and props, appropriate kinds of camera shots, and lighting and musical effects, says Pursell, the director was able to cut many of the play's lines (seen as unnecessary in the visual medium of film) and yet successfully convey its core meanings and feelings.

In each of his Shakespearean films, Zeffirelli offers a lucid and subtle visual interpretation of the particular text. In *The Taming of the Shrew* this is achieved by a very precise balance between apparent authenticity and overt artifice, so that seeing becomes feeling. In *Romeo and Juliet* the balance

From "Artifice and Authenticity in Zeffirelli's *Romeo and Juliet*" by Michael Pursell, *Literature/Film Quarterly*, vol. 14, no. 4 (1986), pp. 173–78. Copyright 1986 by Salisbury State College. Reprinted by permission of the publisher.

is equally precise though its terms are rather different, being informed by the tension announced by the Chorus between the play as history and the play as story.

In Zeffirelli's film, the action starts with a tracking shot of Sampson and Gregory's feet as they pass between the market stalls. This creates at once a sense of penetrable space quite unlike the flat backdrops that open *The Shrew.* Here, it would seem, the dominant mode is to be naturalism. The brilliant red and yellow costumes of the two men seize the eye as their figures are framed through a market stall, while heaps of perfect onions and peppers fill the foreground of the image, their colour carefully chosen to complement the costumes and to stimulate a sensuous engagement with the image. By shooting this with full depth of field, Zeffirelli actively suggests the tangibility of this Verona, creating a compelling amalgam of colour, texture, depth, movement, and sound that draws us irresistibly into the fiction.

This unrestrained, almost fanatical realism, might at first seem to be Zeffirelli's prime concern. The incidental detail authenticates the fictional world, stressing its existence as an autonomous elsewhere, yet it also achieves a fuller resonance. The perfection of the market place becomes, without our really having to think it, a symbol of that order, domesticity and community that the feud constantly threatens. The spectacle of its devastation arising from a grossly anti-social act prefigures, and therefore allows Zeffirelli to trim, Escalus's first speech. Similarly, where Shakespeare begins with a string of Sampson and Gregory's coarse jests, Zeffirelli presents them visually as jesters. Their clothing, like their behaviour, is loud to the point of being offensive. As they begin their talk of quarreling they are momentarily obliterated, visually and aurally, by a cockerel in a cage. This brief image precisely suggests the mindless vanity of their behavior as well as helping to suggest the highly sexed nature of the world we are entering. On a more overt and energetic level, Shakespeare's obscene jokes are replaced by Zeffirelli's first piece of *obviously* careful framing in the film which, by literally underlining it with the bottom frame line, gives noticeable emphasis to Sampson's codpiece as he bites his thumb. Thus, a trivial, minutely authenticating detail of costume is modulated into a visual statement about Sampson and his Verona that completely accords with the written, but here absent, text: He is a young man in love with his own sexual prowess which he expresses through his violence.

This combination of apparently absolute visual and aural authenticity, and the revealing, textually inspired use of detail pervades the film. It is an intense yet clearly controlled naturalism that Zeffirelli offers. That is why the colours of the market produce complement the colours of the characters' costumes. That is why framing is important throughout, particularly since the overall camera style is very fluent, and is thus a persuasive extension of the detailed naturalism within the image. . . .

TYBALT'S DRAMATIC INTRODUCTION

This artful use of authenticity is clear in the scuffles that begin the fight. The hand-held camera presses in close, peering over the shoulders of those in front. This documentary or newsreel technique is reinforced by the absence of music over these shots; the soundtrack consists of a naturalistic amalgam of scuffles, grunts, and cries. Yet if the start of the fight has a documentary quality, its next phase has not. Tybalt's entry is shot from the feet up, and this visual rhyme makes any verbal reference to his allegiance unnecessary. It also reveals what is to become an increasing tension in the film between artifice and authenticity. Tybalt's entry is documentary—the camera first looks at his feet as if the cameraman were momentarily disoriented—but the visual rhyme and the smoothness of the tilt up to his face (again via a prominent codpiece) also make his entry positively ceremonial.

Like all the characters who propel the tragedy directly, Tybalt is introduced in close-ups, in an image that contains a visible tension between the naturalism of the setting and the artifice of the framing, angle, or, in this case, lens. Here the artifice initiated by the visual rhyme (and justifying in retrospect the first shot of Sampson and Gregory) is completed by the telephoto lens. This certainly gives Tybalt added stature and menace by suddenly compressing the space between us and him. More importantly, it announces a stylistic change. The wide-angle lens and hand-held camera of documentary have been replaced by the mounted camera and telephoto lens of conscious fiction. As the visual rhyme implies, Tybalt is about to initiate a resurgence of the violence already begun by Capulet's retainers. The rhyme points to a structured train of events; a sense of structure emphasized by the film's symmetries of composition, controlled colour range and, here, the overt contrast of camera styles. Verona is not an autonomous, historical elsewhere; the authentic detail and prevailing naturalism make it seem so, and it is important that they do. Yet this autonomy is qualified by the conscious and deliberate use of artifice. Verona is a storied world, and it is important that we feel this too.

ROMEO: FROM EYE-LINER TO FACIAL STUBBLE

This accounts for the utterly symmetrical composition of the shot where Romeo is introduced, framed in an arch just as Juliet is first seen framed in a window. The lovers are circumscribed from the moment we see them. This circumscription is part physical—Romeo is seen between high walls, and for him there is no world without Verona walls. It is part social—Juliet is framed in a window of her family mansion, and feels ethically confined by her sense of her father's house; that is why she quite absurdly describes Romeo as her only love sprung from her only hate. The circumscription is narrative too. The lovers are star-cross'd, and their lives are the working out of a pattern first begun by the ancient grudge. They are the proponents of a storied world. That is why the visual style has to change when Romeo first appears. Just as art has to transcend the natural viewpoint in order to create a fictional world of emotional depth, so Zeffirelli's camera moves beyond naturalism at key narrative moments, so that what we see becomes what we feel. This is the visual equivalent of Shakespeare's Chorus, with its emphasis on fatedness and fictionality. The lovers are framed visually but also, by appropriately punning extension, they are framed in the colloquial sense. It is this line of feeling that explains Zeffirelli's meticulous and brilliant handling of the Capulet ball.

It also explains the first close-up of Romeo, which is really quite daring. Dressed in deep lilac, he is obviously a Montagu, having nothing of the Capulet vulgarity and ostentation. Yet this color, the pill-box hat, the obvious eye-liner, the flawless complexion and the flower that just happens to match his doublet suggest falseness and even, perhaps, effeminacy. The former quality is textually substantiated; in his talk of Rosaline, Romeo is shown as a tedious, callow poseur. Zeffirelli relies instead on our visual sense to establish a character in the throes of an early, imaginary love; all verbal reference to Rosaline is cut. As for the effeminacy, in the context of a Verona full of young men whose brains are in their codpieces, Romeo's appearance is like a flush of sympathetic sanity.

In fact, the artificiality of his appearance is part of a larger scheme. It is a commonplace of criticism that Romeo and Juliet mature astonishingly during their brief marriage. We have only to compare Zeffirelli's presentation of Romeo here

ZEFFIRELLI CAPTURES SHAKESPEARE'S SPIRIT

This excerpt from film historian Louis D. Giannetti's Understanding Movies *explains the success of Zeffirelli's rendering of the play by comparing it with the more literal but less colorful 1936 film version by director George Cukor (in which the actors playing Romeo and Juliet were forty-four and thirty-seven, respectively).*

Since plays stress the primacy of language one of the major problems in adapting them for the screen is determining how much of the language is necessary in a predominantly visual art like movies. George Cukor's version of Shakespeare's *Romeo and Juliet* was a conservative film adaptation. Virtually all the dialogue was retained, even the exposition and purely functional speeches of no particular poetic merit. The result was a respectful but often tedious film, in which the visuals tended merely to illustrate the language. Often images and dialogue contained the same information, producing an overblown, static quality that actually contradicted the swift sense of action in the stage play.

Zeffirelli's film version of this play was much more successful. Verbal exposition was cut almost completely and replaced (just as effectively) by visual exposition. Single lines were pruned meticulously if the same information could be conveyed by images. Most of the great poetry was preserved, but often with non-synchronous visuals, to expand—not duplicate—the language. The close-ups looked like a series of exquisite Renaissance portraits. The camera recorded the most intimate details of the lives of the lovers, and the sound-track picked up the most delicate sighs. The fight scenes were more thrilling than any stage presentation could hope to be, for the camera raced and whirled with the combatants. In short, Zeffirelli's movie, though technically less faithful to the stage script, was actually more Shakespearean in spirit than the scrupulously literal version of Cukor.

and in the tomb scene to see this brought out. Yet Romeo's maturing is expressed visually in terms of increasing naturalism and decreasing artifice: from eye-liner to beard stubble, so to speak. At the same time, the pattern of his destiny is working itself out in a movement from naturalism towards artifice, as fate makes tidy conclusions of natural impulses. This is stressed in the choric summation "A glooming peace this morning with it brings. The sun for sorrow will not show his head." Zeffirelli achieves it visually as Romeo falls beside Juliet. He is unshaven and unkempt; her lips are swollen, her face puffy. Yet their dying pose is really just that: a perfectly assumed and composed attitude that declares the fulfillment of the narrative pattern through conscious visual artifice. This double movement in the visual presentation vividly reaffirms the ironies of the drama.

VISIBILITY BECOMES FEELING

To be effective, this tension must be made visible. This need accounts for such early apparent discrepancies as Benvolio's rapidly diminishing wound—an invention of Zeffirelli's which exists solely to draw attention to itself as artifice. Just as Shakespeare is most "artificial" at points of greatest emotional intensity, so too Zeffirelli in III.5 shows Romeo naked and romantically lit. The artifice becomes evident when we reflect that less than twenty-four hours earlier Romeo had fought at length and for his life with Tybalt, yet appears here without a single bruise or blemish. Once again, what we see is what we feel.

The decorum necessary to sustain this kind of balance comes as no surprise after *The Shrew,* and is just as important for this text, being at once so openly artificial and emotionally vivid. The camerawork is a clear response to, and visual reconstruction of, the chorically announced friction in the text between history and story. It is this tension that helps create the emotional perspective of the play and, thanks to Zeffirelli's visual sense, the film. We are visually and emotionally detached from it as history; we are visually and emotionally involved in it as story. Zeffirelli's text literally elucidates Shakespeare's, making it visible. The resulting highly stylized yet emotionally expressive naturalism gives added weight to moments like Juliet's departure from the dance, for example. Her running off is a perfectly natural thing for an over-excited young girl on her first major public occasion. It is also a significant moment in terms of the story, since her physical dizziness represents an emotional disorientation. It is too a prophetic and therefore structural moment that replaces her presentiment in II.2: "I have no joy of this contract tonight / It is too rash; too unadvised; too sudden." Here, as throughout the film, Zeffirelli creates a situation where visibility becomes feeling and feeling becomes awareness.

The entire dance sequence with its combination of spontaneous, effusive emotion and controlled, stylized expression is clearly a visual precursor to the lovers' sonnet dialogue. The choice of sonnet form and the conventional religion-of-love imagery make this dialogue formal to the point of being traditional. This does, of course, generate a pleasant tension between the strict control of the form and the powerful impulses of the emotion beneath. The formal restraint is heard in the regularity of pointing and rhyme and is implicit in such ideas as pilgrimage and saintliness. Romeo's sonnet, for he begins it, is itself therefore an aspect of a whole institutionalised and ritualised process of courtship. It is no surprise to find this sense of tradition in Romeo or Juliet. They are both children of their time and place: Juliet adopts the tribal attitude to Romeo when she first hears his name, while Romeo has already been characterised by his friends and by Capulet as of serious, rather old-fashioned demeanour. The two are heirs to a social context they ignore literally at their peril. Authentic, spontaneous behavior is a dangerous luxury.

THE SINGER BECOMES THE CHORUS

Yet even as they conform to tradition they are breaking it. Their meeting is illicit and hidden. Romeo's comparison of Juliet with a saint brings a youthful sincerity to a rather worn convention. At the same time, the imagery of saints, pilgrims and statues brings with it notions of martyrdom, canonization, immortality and all the fabulous trappings that subtly re-emphasise the storied nature of these authentic emotions and the events they give rise to. Romeo's very sincerity of admiration in all its outdated prolixity is the simultaneous expression of the fate it precipitates. The lovers' speech may be determined by their history—their personalities, their naivete, their uncertainty of each other and their awareness of the social context they find themselves in—but it is also determined by their story. As both a human and a narrative moment, the sonnet dialogue is most effective.

Zeffirelli, however, does not let the text speak entirely for itself. In what might seem simply a concession to the need to popularise, he introduces the song. This consists of a loosely evocative collection of pseudo-Elizabethan sonnet motifs on the themes of the transience of beauty and the imminence of death. This song brackets the sonnet dialogue.

It is clear then that the song provides a storied context for the meeting that is linked with the historical and social context so carefully established in the dance sequence. As the camera locates Romeo and Juliet behind their pillar, the song modulates from [the singer accompanied by a few musicians in the room to an] orchestrated soundtrack score. This orchestration persists throughout the sonnet. Naturalistically, this is absurd, since one is left wondering just what everyone else is doing. It is, of course, a film artifice that is as time-honoured and conventional as Romeo's images of saintliness. We are so used to this that it may not even be consciously perceived as artifice, so that the spectator responds to the whole dialogue-music-kiss monograph as a form of emotionally charged realism. Yet it is the artifice that amplifies the emotion, just as Shakespeare knew when he wrote the sonnet. Besides, the music is not just a vaguely emotive substitute for undramatised feeling as so often in romantic cinema; here it is already charged with the *carpe diem* [make the most of life now] theme of the song from which it originates. . . .

Finally, Zeffirelli concludes the song with the singer looking directly into the camera in a clear violation of the ground rules of cinematic naturalism. The singer addresses us, as no one else in the film is allowed to do. In doing so he momentarily wrests control of visual space from the camera and comments directly on the action, like a documentary reporter. This is somehow less shocking than it ought to be, possibly because the camera angle and costume locate him firmly in Capulet's ball as part of its historicity, before Zeffirelli cuts to a close-up. At all events, the naturalistic convention is not quite broken, though the staring into the camera, like the . . . [orchestrated] modulation of the song, stretches our sense of diegetic [narrative] integrity as far as the dominant naturalism will allow. In this regard, these devices are no different from the symmetrical compositions elsewhere; they are all part of the film's emotionally charged naturalism. Here, of course, Zeffirelli is exploiting the constraints of his medium and his mode: The singer is clearly his version of Shakespeare's Chorus at the beginning of Act II. . . . He takes us into the next Act. The lovers' meeting is part of his song; their poetry is set to his music.

MERGING OF ARTIFICIALITY AND AUTHENTICITY IN THE OPENING SHOT

Zeffirelli opens the film with a similar combination of image, music and text. Visually, he begins with a fade-in to a distant perspective of a city. The shadows and mistiness suggest dawn. Musically, this image is accompanied by a single sombre and cautionary note that leads into the main musical theme. At the same time the Chorus begins to speak, giving precise shape to the musical feeling through voice-over narration. The text is the first eight lines of the Chorus, so that what we hear is simply a direct announcement of the problems to come.

So far, then, it is clearly a storied world. The fade-in is a specifically film convention that introduces a naturalistic image of a town. The presence of music and voice-over are also film artifices as familiar and acceptable to us as the Chorus to an Elizabethan audience. What they announce, as we have seen, is that film conventions are to replace theatrical ones. That is one reason why the Chorus's final six lines are unnecessary.

The images with the music and speech point to the same conclusion, though in more complex ways. Logically, the opening image should be as cinematically conventional . . . as the music and voice-over. The problem is how to do this when naturalism is the desired mode. . . . Zeffirelli solves the problem in an interesting way.

He begins by modulating the naturalism of the opening shot, just as the Chorus in the theatre adjusts our sense of naturalism and authenticity apropos of the events we are to see. The historical aspect of the story is clear enough; it is an ancient grudge that breaks to new mutiny. Yet the present tense of the Chorus's account sits rather oddly with his resume of the lovers' entire life-span. Their story may be from a specific past, but it is to be retold in the present tense, "In fair Verona where we lay our scene."

The events about to unfold thus occupy a *storied* present

tense where Zeffirelli takes some trouble to create in a medium whose naturalistic immediacy threatens to create merely a *virtual* present tense. The difference is crucial. In Shakespeare's Chorus, phrases like "where we lay our scene" are reminders that what we are watching is artifice, however authentic it might momentarily seem. The errors for which he apologises in advance are in this sense merely reminders of that fact, re-emphasising the need for a critical distance between spectator and spectacle. This comes as no surprise in Shakespeare; it does though, hold us off from the total empathic immersion in the events that a virtual present tense encourages. . . .

Zeffirelli [on the other hand] modulates the first image of Verona. Spread out for contemplation, romantically tinted by sunlit mistiness, it is a most evocative image. Yet its function is really to draw attention to itself as an image rather than to establish an environment for the action. Indeed, the action of this story could not take place here, for it is too ambivalent a world.

Despite the light, the accuracy of detail and the perspectives are obviously photographic, and this is reinforced by the better lit sections by the river. Yet the mist blurs the outlines and tints the image to the shade of an aging canvas. The high angle is as much a landscape artist's as a cinematographer's and the lack of motion reinforces the painterly quality. The camera pans right as if to take in the whole work, creating movement just in the way of a documentary film on some aspect of fine art. As the pan proceeds to reveal the true extent of the city straddling its broad river, it becomes clear that despite the effects of mist, angle and stillness, what we are looking at is a photograph of Verona *as it remains now* and as it was then, in the fourteenth or fifteenth centuries. It is the authentic city, presented with conventional photographic naturalism and a degree of photographic artifice. Hovering between snapshot and painting, documentary and fiction, it occupies a . . . space between us and the fiction. Like the Chorus, it is pan of neither world, but gestures at both, reconciling our tense with that of the fiction, our ethical space with that of the film, history with story. Yet, just in case it proves too seductive, the credits over remind us that we are also watching a film and that Franco Zeffirelli is laying the scene. Even so, the "historicised" lettering subtly counteracts even that assertion.

It is a delicate balance, and it announces quite clearly that the film's method will be to combine the authentic with the artificial within the context of a prevailing naturalism. The Chorus's last six lines are thus inappropriate as well as unnecessary.

"Now Art Thou What Thou Art"

Recall the very difficult image of Verona that is presented a few seconds later as the choric voice-over concludes: It is an old, small, walled Italian hill-top town, and remains so throughout the film. It is the antithesis of the opening shot. Here there is motion and bright, clear light. The low camera angle is a cinematographer's, not a painter's, for the motion draws the camera into a pan that leads us to the first shot of the market. It is over this image, with its perfectly ordinary photographic naturalism, that Zeffirelli puts the main title.

It is a major change, for these two images of Verona are simply not compatible as scenes for the action. In fact, the change of viewpoint represents a similar shift in the viewer's emotional perspective. Just as, in the theatre, we attend to the Chorus yet swiftly become involved in the first scene, so here we are advised of the artificial, storied nature of what we are to see, yet are then taken into a highly authentic Verona. . . . The result is that the virtual present is also the storied present; visual space is also ethical space.

We are therefore prepared for the intense, stylised and emotionally expressive naturalism that is to follow, where compositional and other effects seem to rise spontaneously from the photographic authenticity. Mercutio's remark to Romeo is equally appropriate to Zeffirelli's film: "Now art thou what thou art, by art as well as by Nature."

The Play's Spirit Retained in Musical and Artistic Versions

Joseph Kestner

Some of the most popular interpretations of Shake-speare's plays, including *Romeo and Juliet*, have come from the disciplines of music and the fine arts. In this informative essay, first published in the journal *Opera News*, scholar Joseph Kestner discusses some of the great nineteenth- and twentieth-century composers and painters who have been drawn to the tale of the star-crossed lovers. Focusing especially on French composer Charles Gounod's popular 1867 opera based on the play, Kestner explains how Gounod and other artists, while exercising dramatic license in making modest changes, have strived to keep the meaning and spirit of Shakespeare's original work intact.

"I read over this duet, I read it again, I listen to it with all my attention; I try to find it bad, I'm afraid of finding it good and being mistaken! And yet it fired me! It still does! It was born of sincerity. In short, *I believe in it.* Voice, orchestra, everything plays its part; the violins turn passionate, it's all there: Juliet clasping her lover, Romeo's anxiety, his delirious embraces."

So declared [French composer] Charles Gounod on May 2, 1865, about the duet "Nuit d'hyménée" from Act IV of his new opera, *Roméo et Juliette*. Already well known for *Faust* (1859) and *Mireille* (1864), Gounod sensed his greatest moment was coming: the premiere of *Roméo et Juliette* in April 1867 at the Théâtre Lyrique proved a sensation, the only un-qualified success he enjoyed during his lifetime. Since *Roméo et Juliette* was performed the same year as the Expo-sition Universelle [an early "world's fair"], Paris was thronged with foreigners, who carried word back home. It

From "Deathless Love: Across the Centuries, the Romantic Tale of Romeo and Juliet Has Inspired Artists of All Disciplines" by Joseph Kestner, *Opera News*, January 18, 1986, pp. 11–15. ©1986 by the Metropolitan Opera Guild, New York, N.Y. Reprinted by permission of the author and *Opera News*.

was given ninety consecutive performances to packed houses. Gounod's delirium was shared by the world.

Famous lovers are part of the legacy of human culture—Tristan and Isolde, Paolo and Francesca, Hero and Leander, Pyramus and Thisbe, Orpheus and Eurydice, Dido and Aeneas. No pair, however, is more legendary than Romeo Montague and Juliet Capulet, doomed lovers of fourteenth-century Italy. The power of this story has made it extremely attractive to writers, composers and artists. The challenge for Gounod was to create a work good enough to dare the competition. To begin with, there was William Shakespeare.

FOR GOUNOD, SHAKESPEARE'S VERSION WAS BEST

Probably written around 1595, Shakespeare's *Romeo and Juliet* proved extremely popular. Three quartos of varying quality were printed in 1597, 1599 and 1609. The corrupt first quarto of 1597 must have engendered even greater enthusiasm, as the many references after that date attest. Shakespeare's principal and possibly only source was Arthur Brooke's *The Tragicall Historye of Romeus and Juliet* of 1562. . . .

Brooke's key function for Shakespeare, and therefore for Gounod, was in sharpening the characters from other sources [such as Salernitaro's *Il Novellino* and da Porto's *Istoria Novellamente*]. The Nurse becomes an amoral force in the tale; Juliet's parents are etched; Juliet sleeps alone to take the potion; the riot is more developed; Mercutio's nature is embellished. Brooke also introduces the element of Fate or Fortune as a factor in the lovers' destiny. . . . Brooke's *Romeus and Juliet* amalgamated sources for Shakespeare. Shakespeare, however, succeeded in greatly accelerating the story, which in Brooke takes place over a period of months. In Shakespeare the action is compressed to four or five days, lending a breathless, relentless force to the tragic story. And the Bard adds greater passion to the tale by setting it in torrid mid-July.

Shakespeare's *Romeo and Juliet* is a great Renaissance document, celebrating individuality of choice and action. This is emphasized in the play by Romeo's gradual alteration, particularly in three central speeches. In the first scene of Act I ("Love is a smoke made with the fume of sighs"), Romeo speaks with the stereotypical metaphors sanctioned by the tradition of *l'amour courtois* (courtly love).

In the fifth scene, however, after meeting Juliet, Romeo addresses her in the form of the sonnet ("If I profane with my unworthiest hand"), modifying the . . . language of his initial appearance. His transformation to utter individuality occurs in the famous Act II, Scene 2, balcony scene ("But, soft! what light through yonder window breaks? / It is the East, and Juliet is the sun!"). The nature imagery has become totally individualized. His language, now uniquely his own, applies solely to his beloved. The contrast of light and darkness retained by Gounod throughout *Roméo et Juliette,* expresses this radical individualism of the lovers.

THE PLAY AND OPERA COMPARED

Gounod too was concerned with the development of the lovers. The libretto by Jules Barbier and Michel Carré retains the propulsion of the Shakespearean source within the five acts of the opera. Gounod, like Shakespeare, includes a prologue. Writing during the composition of the scene of Juliet's drinking the potion, Gounod remarked about the opera's structure, "The first act ends *brilliantly,* the second is *tender* and *dreamy,* the third *bold* and *animated,* with the duels and Romeo sentenced to exile; the fourth is *dramatic,* the fifth *tragic.* It is a fine progression."

Just as *Romeo and Juliet* is anchored in the three passages transforming Romeo's language of love, *Roméo et Juliette* is constructed around four love duets. The first, "Ange adorable," based on the sonnet "If I profane" from the play, is suitable in its formality for the first meeting. Act II begins with Roméo's aria "Ah! lève-toi, soleil," derived from Shakespeare's Act II, Scene 2 ("It is the East, and Juliet is the sun! / Arise, fair sun, and kill the envious moon"). Gounod's structure therefore follows Shakespeare's emphasis on the lovers' independence from stereotypical emotion. In the duet in Act II ("O nuit divine!") the lovers' separation from the world begins as they plan their wedding. As in Shakespeare, Gounod's Roméo transforms his language into Juliette herself ("Sois l'aurore"). The Act IV duet, "Nuit d'hyménée" individualizes the lovers in their language ("Le ciel rayonne en moi"). The final duet, "Console-toi, pauvre âme," evokes the lark/nightingale motif from the marriage-night episode in Shakespeare.

Gounod is very much a part of his time in this final episode, where Roméo and Juliette sing together before their death. In Shakespeare, Romeo is dead before Juliet awakens, but eighteenth- and nineteenth-century audiences would not tolerate such a scene without some farewell words exchanged by the lovers. This tradition is based on [actor-manager] David Garrick's 1761 play-text of Shakespeare, which included the final dialogue in the tomb. After Romeo takes the poison, Juliet awakens asking, "Where am I?" Romeo exclaims, "She speaks, she lives!" The lovers discourse about their future until the poison seizes Romeo. Juliet stabs herself, as in Gounod. Gounod also follows Garrick in cutting the appearance of the fathers and their reconciliation, bringing down the curtain with Juliet's suicide.

OTHER MUSICAL VERSIONS OF THE STAR-CROSSED LOVERS

During the nineteenth century, the legend of Romeo and Juliet became increasingly popular in music and art. Gounod's *Roméo et Juliette* is part of a continuous operatic and orchestral interest in the lovers. Treatments by forgotten composers such as Nicola Zingarelli (1796) and Nicola Vaccai (1825) might have posed no threat, but Gounod's opera was competing with Vincenzo Bellini's *I Capuleti e i Montecchi*, premiered in 1830. . . .

The differences between the Bellini and the Gounod are significant. The two leads in Bellini are a soprano and mezzo-soprano; Lorenzo is a doctor rather than a friar; Romeo has slain Capulet's son before the opera commences; Tebaldo [the equivalent of Tybalt] is betrothed to Giulietta and is not slain by Romeo; no Nurse or Mercutio is included. As Bellini's title indicates, the ambience of *I Capuleti e i Montecchi* is martial and warlike. The lovers are representatives of the two houses, whose political strife . . . is emphasized throughout. . . . In Bellini the city of Verona is violent, almost anarchic. Giulietta from the beginning is filled with doom. So chaotic is the universe that the lovers are never even married.

When still a young man, Gounod had heard Hector Berlioz' dramatic symphony *Roméo et Juliette* (1839), a work Berlioz described as "neither an opera in concert form nor a cantata, but a symphony with chorus." Berlioz' work draws its inspiration from Garrick, whose version he had seen performed in 1827 . . . evoking in the music the elements of Garrick's additional final scene (Romeo's suicide, the lovers' brief dialogue and Juliet's end). Though Garrick cut the reconciliation of the Montagues and Capulets, Berlioz includes a lengthy scene for Père Laurence [the friar], who denounces the violence of the families and compels their reconciliation, as in Shakespeare. Gounod's opera preceded by two years Tchaikovsky's fantasy-overture *Romeo and Juliet,* first heard in 1870. Heavily revised in 1872 and in 1880, the overture begins with ecclesiastical harmonies suggesting Friar Laurence, passes to the street fight and then to the lovers and concludes with a tempestuous coda evoking their doom.

In the twentieth century, three compositions have been inspired by the legend. With *A Village Romeo and Juliet* (1907)

THE LAST ACT OF GOUNOD'S OPERA

This synopsis of act 5 of Gounod's Roméo et Juliette, *from Milton Cross's popular book* Complete Stories of the Great Operas, *illustrates the changes the composer made in Shakespeare's original, including having Romeo die after Juliet awakens and cutting the final reconciliation scene with the parents.*

The burial vault of the Capulets. Juliette, in her deathlike slumber, lies on a bier in the center of the chamber. After a brief prelude in the form of an instrumental chorale there is a scene before the curtain, in which Friar Laurence is informed by Friar Jean that Roméo's page was attacked and wounded by the Capulets while on his way to deliver the message explaining about the potion. Friar Laurence immediately dispatches Friar Jean in all haste to Roméo.

There is a brief orchestral interlude, wonderfully descriptive of Juliette's sleep. Roméo enters the tomb, gazes upon his bride, whom he believes to be dead, and marvels that even death has not robbed her of her loveliness ("Salut! tombeau! sombre et silencieux"). In a transport of grief he embraces Juliette and then drinks poison from a vial he has brought with him. As he slowly succumbs Juliette revives. Bewildered and unbelieving, they greet each other and in a poignant refrain ("Dieu de bonté!") give thanks for their reunion.

Juliette cries out in alarm at Roméo's sudden paroxysm of agony. He gasps that he took poison because he believed her to be dead. As approaching death clouds his mind, Roméo recalls, in the refrain of the farewell duet, their tender words about the lark and the nightingale. Frenziedly Juliette asks if there is no poison left for her. Crying out that there is another way, she draws a dagger from the folds of her gown and plunges it into her breast. With a final prayer for forgiveness ("Seigneur, pardonnez-nous") Roméo and Juliette die in each other's arms. The curtain falls.

British composer Frederick Delius drew his inspiration from the novella *Romeo und Julia auf dem Dorfe,* written by Gottfried Keller in 1856. The opera recounts the tragedy of Sali and Vreli, son and daughter of rival farmers. The lovers have a wedding only in a dream, achieving a brief union on a barge, which they intentionally sink in mutual suicide.... The Italian Riccardo Zandonai, best known for *Francesca da Rimini* (1914), composed *Giulietta e Romeo,* which received its premiere in 1921. Like the Bellini, Zandonai's opera presents a violent world. The lovers have been secretly married before the action begins. Preserving the imagery of Shakespeare, the first act moves from darkness to daylight. As in Gounod, the lovers have a brief dialogue before their death.... The most recent distinguished realization of the Romeo and Juliet idea is in Sergei Prokofiev's ballet introduced in 1938. The first Soviet performance of the ballet took place in 1940, with choreography by Leonid Lavrovsky.

ROMEO AND JULIET CAPTURED ON CANVAS

Visual interest in the legend of Romeo and Juliet reached its peak during the late eighteenth century and in the middle and late nineteenth, particularly in England. In the late eighteenth century the publisher John Boydell conceived the idea of a Shakespeare Gallery, which would exhibit paintings of Shakespearean scenes. The Gallery opened in May 1789 with thirty-four canvases; additions increased the total to over 150 by the time the collection was sold in 1805. Some of the most preeminent artists of the time exhibited in the Gallery. James Northcote completed (1792) a tomb scene, showing Juliet dismissing the Friar as Romeo and Paris lie slain at her feet. John Opie's *Juliet in the Trance* (1791) is based on Act IV, the presumed death of Juliet. William Miller finished a canvas of Romeo and Juliet in eighteenth-century dress for the famous touching of hands in Act I.

Two canvases from the period not completed for Boydell are particularly noteworthy. Matthew William Peters (1742–1814) depicted the suicide of Juliet ("O happy dagger"), ... with Romeo lying in her lap as she raises the fatal weapon. Peters focuses on the incident that ended the play in Garrick. In 1809 the Swiss-born Henry Fuseli completed *Romeo Slaying Paris at the Bier of Juliet* from Act V. Romeo thrusts his sword at Paris as Juliet lies between them, the dynamism of Fuseli's conception enhanced by the Shakespearean contrast of darkness and light. In 1836 J.M.W. Turner exhibited *Juliet and Her Nurse,* showing Juliet gazing over the Piazza San Marco in Venice. The French artist Eugene Delacroix in 1846 showed the two lovers embracing after their wedding night as Romeo prepares to go into exile in Mantua.

The story of Romeo and Juliet became especially popular in British painting from midcentury onward. Several factors contributed to this interest. The art critic John Ruskin published his monumental study *The Stones of Venice* between 1851 and 1853, evoking the glory of Italy while chronicling its demise. Politics also renewed interest in Italy, especially the events surrounding the Risorgimento, the movement to unify Italy and free it from Austrian domination. . . .

The young Pre-Raphaelite artist John Everett Millais painted *The Death of Romeo and Juliet* (c. 1848), showing the two lovers clutched in an embrace while the families rush into the tomb. In 1853 William Grant exhibited *Juliet and the Friar* from Act IV, a theme not frequently portrayed; Juliet appears cautious, the Friar aged and beneficent. Frederic Leighton, who had studied in Italy and preferred Shakespeare's Italian dramas, depicted incidents from the drama three times. The first, *The Duel Between Romeo and Tybalt* (1850), is untraced. In 1855 Leighton exhibited *The Reconciliation of the Montagues and the Capulets over the Dead Bodies of Romeo and Juliet.* The Prince stands between Capulet on the left and Montague on the right, who points to the corpses of the lovers; Lady Capulet has thrown herself over their bodies, and Paris lies dead beside them. The rich coloring of the canvas evokes the mystery and splendor of the Italian Middle Ages. In his 1858 canvas *The Feigned Death of Juliet,* Leighton depicts Count Paris arriving for his marriage and discovering his bride "dead." Leighton distills the varied reactions of the characters around the bed, from the old Nurse to the Friar.

A particularly poignant theme that attracted artists was the parting of Romeo and Juliet after their wedding night, from Act III. The Pre-Raphaelite artist Ford Madox Brown completed a richly colored version in 1870, showing Romeo kissing Juliet passionately before he descends, as dawn breaks over the city. Brown captures the tension by the foot in the rope ladder and Romeo's extended arm. To recreate the atmosphere of Italy, Brown had borrowed photographs from his colleague Dante Gabriel Rossetti, whose father had come as a political exile from Italy in 1825. In 1884 Frank Dicksee, one of the later great Victorian painters, also depicted the lovers parting.

A Tradition of "Deathless Love"

The legend of Romeo and Juliet became a powerful symbol in the nineteenth century for musicians and artists. The defiant love ethic of these two characters paralleled the reformist political impulse of the century and confirmed the individualism of nineteenth-century romantic self-assertion. Gounod's *Roméo et Juliette* is part of a cultural legacy including composers from Bellini to Zandonai and artists from Fuseli to Dicksee. "Never was a story of more woe / Than this of Juliet and her Romeo." As this extensive tradition demonstrates, the love depicted in *Roméo et Juliette* has become more deathless than ever.

Chronology

1476

Italian writer Masuccio of Salerno's *Il Novellino*, containing a story similar to *Romeo and Juliet*, appears.

1530

Italian writer Luigi da Porto's *Istoria Novellamente*, based on Masuccio's work, sets the story of the ill-fated lovers in Verona, Italy, and introduces such elements as the balcony scene and the name of the male lover—Romeo.

1543

Polish astronomer Nicolaus Copernicus introduces the idea of a sun- rather than earth-centered universe in his *On the Revolutions*.

1557

William Shakespeare's parents, John Shakespeare and Mary Arden, are married.

1558

Elizabeth I becomes queen of England, initiating the so-called Elizabethan age.

1561

The great Elizabethan writer Francis Bacon is born.

1562

English poet Arthur Brooke publishes his long poem *The Tragical History of Romeus and Juliet*, Shakespeare's source for his play version of the lovers' story.

1564

William Shakespeare is born in the village of Stratford in central England; his noted contemporary, writer Christopher Marlowe, is also born.

1572

Playwright Ben Jonson, who will later become a rival of Shakespeare's, is born.

1576

London's first public theater, called the Theatre, opens.

1577

Raphael Holinshed's *Chronicles*, the source for many of Shakespeare's plays, appears.

1577–1580

Englishman Sir Francis Drake sails around the world.

1582

William Shakespeare marries Anne Hathaway.

1585

Shakespeare's twins, Hamnet and Judith, are born.

CA. 1587

Shakespeare leaves Stratford and heads for London to pursue a career in the theater.

1588

England wins a major victory over Spain by defeating the mighty Spanish Armada.

CA. 1590–1593

Shakespeare writes *Richard III*; *The Comedy of Errors*; and *Henry VI, Parts 1, 2,* and *3.*

1594

Shakespeare joins the newly formed Lord Chamberlain's Men theatrical company.

CA. 1594–1600

Shakespeare writes *The Taming of the Shrew*; *The Two Gentlemen of Verona*; *The Merry Wives of Windsor*; *Twelfth Night*; *Richard II*; *Henry IV, Parts 1* and *2*; *Henry V*; and *Julius Caesar.*

CA. 1595

Shakespeare composes *Romeo and Juliet.*

1597

Shakespeare buys New Place, the largest home in Stratford; the First Quarto, or early printed edition, of *Romeo and Juliet* appears.

1598–1599

The Globe Theatre opens; Shakespeare owns one-eighth of its profits.

1599

The Second Quarto of *Romeo and Juliet* is printed.

1600

In Italy, the church burns priest Giordano Bruno at the stake for advocating the idea that the stars are distant suns, each having its own planets.

CA. 1601–1607

Shakespeare writes what will later be acknowledged as his greatest tragedies, *Hamlet, Othello, King Lear, Macbeth,* and *Antony and Cleopatra.*

1603

Queen Elizabeth dies; James I becomes king of England; the English conquer Ireland.

1607

English settlers establish the colony of Jamestown in North America.

CA. 1608–1613

Shakespeare writes *Coriolanus, The Winter's Tale, Henry VIII,* and *The Two Noble Kinsmen.*

1609

The Third Quarto of *Romeo and Juliet* appears.

1610

Italian scholar Galileo Galilei points his newly built telescope at the planet Jupiter and discovers four orbiting moons, proving conclusively that all heavenly bodies do not revolve around Earth.

1611

The King James Version of the Bible is published.

1616

Shakespeare dies.

1623

Anne Hathaway Shakespeare dies; the First Folio, a complete collection of Shakespeare's works, is published.

1935

Acclaimed British actors Laurence Olivier and John Gielgud alternate the roles of Romeo and Mercutio in a London stage production of *Romeo and Juliet* that boasts the longest continuous run of performances of the play on record.

1936

The first major film version of *Romeo and Juliet*, directed by George Cukor, is released.

1957

The musical play *West Side Story*, based on *Romeo and Juliet*, opens on Broadway in New York City.

1968

Director Franco Zeffirelli releases his highly acclaimed film version of *Romeo and Juliet.*

1996

The most recent film version of Shakespeare's play about the star-crossed lovers is released, the setting updated to the present-day United States.

FOR FURTHER RESEARCH

SHAKESPEARE'S LIFE AND TIMES

Gerald E. Bentley, *Shakespeare: A Biographical Handbook.* Westport, CT: Greenwood, 1986.

Marchette Chute, *Shakespeare of London.* New York: E.P. Dutton, 1949.

Roland M. Frye, *Shakespeare's Life and Times: A Pictorial Record.* Princeton: Princeton University Press, 1967.

François Laroque, *The Age of Shakespeare.* New York: Harry N. Abrams, 1993.

————, *Shakespeare's Festive World: Elizabethan Seasonal Entertainment and the Professional Stage.* New York: Cambridge University Press, 1991.

Peter Levi, *The Life and Times of William Shakespeare.* New York: Henry Holt, 1989.

Peter Quennell, *Shakespeare: A Biography.* Cleveland: World Publishing Company, 1963.

A.L. Rowse, *Shakespeare: A Biography.* New York: Harper and Row, 1963.

————, *Shakespeare the Man.* New York: Harper and Row, 1973.

Edith Sitwell, *A Notebook on William Shakespeare.* Boston: Beacon Press, 1948.

SHAKESPEAREAN THEATER AND FILM

John C. Adams, *The Globe Playhouse: Its Design and Equipment.* Cambridge, MA: Harvard University Press, 1942.

Sally Beauman, *The Royal Shakespeare Company: A History of Ten Decades.* Oxford: Oxford University Press, 1982.

Donald Brook, *A Pageant of English Actors.* New York: Macmillan, 1950.

Ivor Brown, *Shakespeare and the Actors.* New York: Coward McCann, 1970.

Cecil De Banke, *Shakespeare Production, Then and Now.* London: Hutchinson, 1954.

Charles W. Eckert, *Focus on Shakespearean Films.* Englewood Cliffs, NJ: Prentice-Hall, 1972.

John Elsom, *Post-War British Theater Criticism.* London: Routledge and Kegan Paul, 1981.

John Gielgud, *An Actor and His Times.* London: Sidgwick and Jackson, 1979.

Gordon Grosse, *Shakespearean Playgoing, 1890–1952.* London: Mowbray, 1953.

G.B. Harrison, *Elizabethan Plays and Players.* Ann Arbor: University of Michigan Press, 1956.

Anthony Holden, *Laurence Olivier: A Biography.* New York: Atheneum, 1988.

Roger Manvell, *Shakespeare and the Film.* London: Debt, 1971.

Garry O'Connor, *Ralph Richardson: An Actor's Life.* London: Hodder and Stoughton, 1982.

Laurence Olivier, *On Acting.* London: Weidenfeld and Nicolson, 1986.

Robert Speaight, *Shakespeare on the Stage.* London: Collins, 1973.

Arthur C. Sprague, *Shakespeare and the Actor's Stage Business in His Plays (1660–1905).* Cambridge, MA: Harvard University Press, 1944.

Peter Whitehead and Robin Bean, *Olivier: Shakespeare.* London: Lorrimer Films, 1966.

GENERAL SHAKESPEAREAN ANALYSIS AND CRITICISM

Isaac Asimov, *Asimov's Guide to Shakespeare.* New York: Avenel Books, 1978.

Andrew C. Bradley, *Shakespearean Tragedy.* New York: Viking Penguin, 1991.

John R. Brown and Bernard Harris, eds., *Early Shakespeare.* New York: Schocken Books, 1966.

Edmund K. Chambers, *William Shakespeare: A Study of Facts and Problems.* New York: Oxford University Press, 1989.

Samuel T. Coleridge, *Lectures and Notes on Shakespeare.* London: Oxford University Press, 1931.

John W. Draper, *Stratford to Dogberry: Studies in Shakespeare's Earlier Plays.* Freeport, NY: Books for the Libraries Press, 1970.

William Empson, *Essays on Shakespeare.* New York: Cambridge University Press, 1986.

Brian Gibbons, *Shakespeare and Multiplicity.* Cambridge, England: Cambridge University Press, 1993.

Harley Granville-Barker and G.B. Harrison, eds., *A Companion to Shakespeare Studies.* Cambridge, England: Cambridge University Press, 1959.

Brander Matthews and Ashley H. Thorndike, eds., *Shakespearean Studies by Members of the Department of English and Comparative Literature in Columbia University.* New York: Russell and Russell, 1962.

Dieter Mehl, *Shakespeare's Tragedies: An Introduction.* New York: Cambridge University Press, 1986.

Kenneth Muir and Samuel Schoenbaum, eds., *A New Companion to Shakespeare Studies.* Oxford: Oxford University Press, 1971.

Paul N. Siegel, ed., *His Infinite Variety: Major Shakespearean Criticism Since Jonson.* Philadelphia: J.B. Lippincott, 1964.

Clarice Swisher, ed., *Readings on Shakespeare: The Tragedies.* San Diego: Greenhaven Press, 1996.

Edwin Wilson, ed., *Shaw on Shakespeare: An Anthology of Bernard Shaw's Writings on the Plays and Production of Shakespeare.* Freeport, NY: Books for the Libraries Press, 1971.

TEXT AND CRITICISM OF *ROMEO AND JULIET*

David Atkinson, "*Romeo and Juliet*, V.i.24," *Notes and Queries*, March 1988, pp. 49–52.

David M. Bergeron, "Sickness in *Romeo and Juliet*," *CLA Journal*, March 1977, pp. 356–64.

James C. Bryant, "The Problematic Friar in *Romeo and Juliet*," *English Studies*, August 1974, pp. 340–50.

Bert Cardullo, "The Friar's Flaw, the Play's Tragedy: The Experiment of *Romeo and Juliet*," *CLA Journal*, June 1985, pp. 404–14.

W.C. Carroll, "We Are Born to Die," *Comparative Drama*, Spring 1981, pp. 54–71.

Jill Colaco, "The Window Scenes in *Romeo and Juliet* and Folk Songs of the Night Visit," *Studies in Philology*, Spring 1986, pp. 138–57.

Ann J. Cook, *Making a Match: Courtship in Shakespeare and His Society*. Princeton: Princeton University Press, 1991.

T.J. Cribb, "The Unity of *Romeo and Juliet*," *Shakespeare Survey*, vol. 34, 1981, pp. 93–104.

Barbara Hodgdon, "Absent Bodies, Present Voices: Performance Work and the Close of *Romeo and Juliet*'s Golden Story," *Theater Journal*, October 1989, pp. 341–59.

Joan O. Holmer, "'Myself Condemned and Myself Excus'd': Tragic Effects in *Romeo and Juliet*," *Studies in Philology*, Summer 1991, pp. 345–62.

———, "Draw If You Be Men," *Shakespeare Quarterly*, Summer 1994, pp. 163–89.

G.K. Hunter, "Shakespeare's Earliest Tragedies: *Titus Andronicus* and *Romeo and Juliet*," *Shakespeare Survey*, vol. 27, 1974, pp. 1–9.

Joseph Kestner, "Deathless Love," *Opera News*, January 18, 1986, pp. 11–15.

Kathleen E. McLuskie, "Shakespeare's 'Earth-Treading Stars': The Image of the Masque in *Romeo and Juliet*," *Shakespeare Survey*, vol. 24, 1971, pp. 63–69.

Giorgio Melchiori, "Peter, Balthasar, and Shakespeare's Art of Doubling," *Modern Language Review*, October 1983, pp. 777–92.

E. Pearlman, "Staging *Romeo and Juliet*: Evidence from Brooke's *Romeus*," *Theater Survey*, May 1993, pp. 22–32.

Roger Prior, "'Runnawayes Eyes': A Genuine Crux," *Shakespeare Quarterly*, Summer 1989, pp. 191–95.

Michael Pursell, "Artifice and Authenticity in Zeffirelli's

Romeo and Juliet," Literature/Film Quarterly, vol. 13, no. 4, 1986, pp. 173–79.

J. Rees, "Juliet's Nurse," *English Studies*, February 1983, pp. 43–47.

Amy J. Riess and George W. Williams, "'Tragical Mirth': From *Romeo* to *Dream*," *Shakespeare Quarterly*, Summer 1992, pp. 214–18.

R. Stamm, "The First Meeting of the Lovers in Shakespeare's *Romeo and Juliet*," *English Studies*, February 1986, pp. 2–13.

Leslie Thomson, "'With patient ears attend': *Romeo and Juliet* on the Elizabethan Stage," *Studies in Philology*, Spring 1995, pp. 230–47.

Louis B. Wright and Virginia A. LaMar, eds., *Romeo and Juliet*, by William Shakespeare. New York: Washington Square Press, 1959.

INDEX